How Can Digital Technologies Improve Public Services and Governance?

How Can Digital Technologies Improve Public Services and Governance?

Nagy K. Hanna

BUSINESS EXPERT PRESS

How Can Digital Technologies Improve Public Services and Governance?
Copyright © Business Expert Press, LLC, 2017.

First published in 2017 by
Business Expert Press, LLC
222 East 46th Street, New York, NY 10017
www.businessexpertpress.com

ISBN-13: 978-1-63157-813-7 (paperback)
ISBN-13: 978-1-63157-814-4 (e-book)

Business Expert Press Service Systems and Innovations in Business and Society Collection

Collection ISSN: 2326-2664 (print)
Collection ISSN: 2326-2699 (electronic)

Cover and interior design by S4Carlisle Publishing Services Private Ltd., Chennai, India

First edition: 2017

10 9 8 7 6 5 4 3 2 1

Printed in the United States of America.

Abstract

Citizens are demanding more openness, transparency, and accountability for public services, and this demand has been heightened by the growing economic inequality and insecurity in many developed and developing countries. State performance remains disappointingly poor in many parts of the world, putting at risk the further progress on development goals. Governance and public sector capacity are thus the major building blocks of the development strategy of emerging economies.

Meantime, digital technologies such as mobile are sweeping the planet—inducing power shifts and posing profound implications and opportunities for accountability to citizens and for continuous service innovation. While the pace of this shift may be uncertain, the long-term impact is likely to be profound.

The book considers the opportunities and challenges of harnessing digital technologies for improved public services and governance. It focuses on the challenges of applying digital technologies in developing countries, where dramatic results can be realized. It addresses questions like these: How can digital technologies help enhance transparency, accountability, and participation to improve service design and delivery? Where are the opportunities to enhance key areas of governance and public service delivery? What are the promising practices to strengthen supply and mobilize demand for good governance and service delivery? What are the emerging lessons from recent experience?

The author shows through many examples how information and communication technology (ICT) can be deployed to improve public sector efficiency and accountability for resource management; improve access and quality of public services for citizens; enhance transparency and reduce costs of government–business transactions, support entrepreneurship, attract private investment, and reduce the burden of regulation; and enhance the effectiveness of political oversight and policy institutions. The author also shows the crucial importance of understanding the social, political, institutional, informational, and stakeholder contexts for ICT to strengthen demand for good governance.

It is hoped that the many examples provided in this book can contribute to our understanding of how to integrate ICT into efforts to enhance the capacity of citizens to hold their governments accountable and to ease governance challenges. The aim of the author is to raise awareness about the potential and current state of digital technologies as a means to transform public services and enhance government accountability and civic participation in governance. He also underlines the importance of the policies and institutions that might sustain and scale up ICT for governance and public service improvement. He points to the opportunities and challenges in pursuing public sector transformation. In doing so, he provides clear guidelines for stakeholders and a basis for policy dialogue within governments and with service providers, development partners, and civil society, seeking to create enabling environments for responsive service delivery and good governance.

Keywords

Access to public services, Citizen empowerment, Corruption, Demand for good governance (DFGG), Developing countries, Digital innovation, Digital technologies, Digital transformation, information and communication technology (ICT), Governance, Internet, Open data, Open government, Open innovation, Political governance, Social accountability (social control), Transparency, Public service delivery, Public service innovation.

Contents

Acknowledgments

This original study on which this book is based was commissioned by the World Bank. It focused on providing guidance to development professionals as they assist their client countries in the challenging area of governance and public services improvement. It benefitted from comments by many World Bank officials: Roberto O. Panzardi, Laurent Besancon, Anand Rajaram, Philippe Dongier, Immanuel Steinhilper, Shilpa Banerji, Helene Grandvoinnet, Motoky Hayakawa, Maria Amelina, Mary McNeil, Samia Melhem, Adrian Fozzard, Gaurav Relhan.

The original study was also funded by the generous support of the Governance Partnership Facility (GPF), a multi-donor trust fund financed by the United Kingdom (DFID), the Ministry of Foreign Affairs of the Netherlands, and Norway to support innovative work on governance in the World Bank.

Special thanks to two reviewers: Lucienne Abrahams, Director of LINK Centre, University of the Witwatersrand; and James Spohrer, IBM Research Director. I also much appreciate the comments and advice of the three academics who provided blind reviews, as required by University of the Witwatersrand for academic publications. These reviewers diligently and generously provided extensive comments as well as encouragement.

Adapting the study findings into a concise book for policy makers, public service providers, and development professionals for the *Business Expert Press* was the idea of James Spohrer. Scott Isenberg, executive acquisition editor, took this idea further and with enthusiasm. Rene Caroline provided excellent copy-editing and book production.

Abbreviations and Acronyms

CSO	Civil society organization
CSR	Corporate social responsibility
DFGG	Demand for Good Governance
e-GP	e-government procurement
GIC	Government Information Center
ICT	Information and communication technology
IFMIS	Integrated Financial Management and Information System
IFMSs	Integrated Financial Management Systems
IM	Instant messaging
ISP	Internet service provider
IT	Information technology
M&E	Monitoring and evaluation
	m-application mobile-phone application
M-Pesa	Mobile-based money transaction service in Kenya (*pesa* means "money" in Swahili)
NeGP	National e-Governance Plan
NGO	Nongovernmental organization
OECD	Organization for Economic Co-operation and Development
OGP	Open Government Partnership
PPPs	Public–private partnerships
SIs	Social intermediaries
SIM	Subscriber Identity Module
SMEs	Small and medium enterprises
UID	Unique Identification
UNDESA	United Nations Department of Economic and Social Affairs

CHAPTER 1

Opportunities and Challenges Overview

All over the world, citizens are demanding more openness, transparency, and accountability for public services, and this demand has been heightened since the 2008 global financial crisis, the Arab Spring Uprisings of 2011, and growing economic insecurity in many developed and developing countries. Citizens are becoming increasingly vocal in their dissatisfaction with corruption, rising inequality, poor service delivery, and public policy formulation and execution. They are seeking to monitor public sector performance, services, budgets, and programs, challenging government performance, and influencing policy decisions, through the new social media, and mobile apps, among others. Progressive policy makers and service providers are also seeking client feedback and coinnovation and cocreation of services. Development thinkers and practitioners have increasingly acknowledged the centrality of governance and improved public services to accelerated and sustainable development (Acemoglu and Robinson 2012; World Bank 2003 and 2017). While demand for good governance is emerging as a priority in the international development community, much still needs to be done to ensure its adaptation to the context of developing countries and poor communities.

In the meantime, a number of new digital technologies (information and communication technologies, or ICTs) are sweeping the planet—inducing power shifts and posing profound implications and opportunities for transparency, governance, and accountability to citizens (social accountability), and for continuous service improvement and innovation. Mobile phones have diffused rapidly in poor and rich countries alike, and now offer high access and mobility, and a ubiquitous platform for easy-to-develop applications for networking, collecting data, monitoring projects, and reporting misdeeds. Crowdsourcing technology is enabling collaboration in real time and on a massive scale, including service innovation. Geo-mapping technologies, big data, and analytics can now help governments, citizens, and social intermediaries to overlay socioeconomic information with geospatial data—pinpointing the distribution of projects and their impact, enabling active citizen participation in solving local problems, and so on. Advances in databases, broadband, cloud computing, and open data platforms are enabling data sharing and opening up massive government data stores to citizens and businesses—with major implications for open government, and coproduction and collaborative innovation of services. The open government data initiative that the United States pioneered a few years ago is being adapted and replicated in many advanced as well as developing countries.

The book considers the opportunities and challenges of harnessing digital technologies for improved public services and governance. It focuses on the challenges of applying digital technologies in developing countries, particularly in Africa, where dramatic results can be realized. It focuses on ways to improve services beyond supply-side measures such as business-process-engineering and improved management of service providers. Thus, it focuses on strengthening the demand for good governance and improved services via informed citizens, client feedback, and enhanced monitoring of service provider performance. It addresses questions like these: How can digital technologies help enhance transparency, accountability, and participation to improve service design and delivery? What are the broad ICT application opportunities to enhance key areas of governance and public service delivery? What practices have been seen to strengthen supply and mobilize demand for good governance? How could policy reform and other complementary investments in technology, institutions, and capabilities at the national and local levels have maximum impact on ICT for service delivery? What are the promises and limits of digital technologies for service delivery? What are the emerging lessons from recent experience? What are the promising areas for future action, experimentation, and research? And what are the risks to privacy and security arising from increased access to information about citizens?

Opportunities for Governance and Innovation in Public Servcies

Digital technologies allow citizens to adopt new strategies to communicate, coordinate, mobilize, and have their voices heard. Digital networks have acted as a massive supply shock to the spread and cost of information, including information on government programs and performance. They also made it possible for citizens to make their voices heard, by increasing their reach and access to media. In the process, they magnify the speed and scale of group coordination and help synchronize the behavior of groups quickly, cheaply, and publicly in ways that were unavailable as recently as a decade ago. ICT can empower citizens and businesses to access, coproduce, and utilize information to hold public agencies accountable for enforcing laws and delivering public services, and to participate meaningfully in managing development. Trends in connectivity, mobile phones, and ICT platforms suggest that ICT will increasingly become a transformative tool for governance, by making government processes transparent and information accessible to all stakeholders. Digital technologies offer powerful tools and platforms for addressing development challenges in general, and public sector performance and governance in particular (Chapter 2). They both require and offer the opportunity to rethink the process by which the state and nonstate actors interact to design and implement policies and public services.

The book shows through many examples how ICT can be deployed to *improve public sector efficiency and accountability for resource management* by: modernizing public expenditure management systems, making them transparent, and tracking budgets online and through mobile devices (Chapter 3). Digital technologies can help make public services more inclusive by mapping and monitoring the needs and resources of poor communities with mobile and digital mapping technologies. E-government procurement can open up public procurement systems for fair competition and accountability by using electronic procurement applications and engaging social intermediaries. Integrated financial management systems can modernize tax systems and revenue administration to raise revenues while reducing corruption, tax avoidance, and misallocation of expenditures. Human resources management systems can improve public service performance by using incentives tied to clear and measurable performance indicators and service outcomes.

ICT can be applied to improve the supply of each public service or function and at the same time strengthen transparency, accountability, and demand for continuous improvement and good governance. Optimally used, ICT can modernize and reengineer government processes (to make resource management more efficient and responsive, for example), and at the same time render them transparent, enable oversight, and strengthen social accountability. In the area of corruption, a key is to make information more readily available; for instance, by putting corruption-prone activities online and making them monitorable and searchable.

A second broad area of ICT-enabled governance is *services to citizens* (Chapter 3). Improving public service access and quality is a political, social, and economic imperative for all developing countries, and particularly for many African countries that have persistently low human development indicators. The UN consensus on Sustainable Development Goals sets even more ambitious targets for eradicating poverty and shared prosperity by 2030. A key route to improve the availability, quality and responsiveness of public services is to augment citizen monitoring and feedback. This is perhaps the most fertile area for using ICT to strengthen accountability via citizens and social intermediaries, using mobile, e-government, and open data. The book surveys applications in Africa, ranging from the supply of water, land titles, licenses, permits, and certificates via citizen-centric portals and community access centers, to the delivery and monitoring of health and education services, to providing choice and competition in service delivery through information brokerage and the use of public–private partnerships (PPPs).

A third area is to *enhance transparency and reduce costs of government—business transactions*, support entrepreneurship and small enterprise development, attract private investment, facilitate trade, and reduce the burden of regulation. This is a crucial area for the future of developing countries with its potential for employment generation, competitiveness, and broad-based growth. Relevant transactions and services cover customs, public procurement, online business registration and permits, access to land records, municipal services to business, financial services (including mobile-based transactions), monitoring of agricultural and other extension services, and monitoring government enforcement of regulation. Although there are promising grassroots innovations in this area, they lag behind ICT use for government accountability to provide services to citizens. This is perhaps due to conflicting interests and weak partnerships among business intermediaries, development partners, and nongovernmental organizations (NGOs).

One final broad area in which ICT can improve governance is to *enhance the effectiveness and accountability of political, oversight, and policy institutions*; enforce the rule of law; and modernize the legislative and judicial branches of government (Chapter 3). For example, ICT can improve parliamentary processes in many ways—improving transparency and openness; providing information access to citizens; improving the mechanisms of accountability of legislators to their electorates; enabling dialogue between the parliament, its members, and the citizenry; and helping citizens keep an eye on parliament. Other examples include monitoring elections and crowdsourcing data from citizens on violence, human rights abuses, and crisis situations, and enhancing the capacity and transparency of policy-making and oversight institutions.

The impact of digital technology on citizen empowerment and government (and provider) capability depends on the initial strengths of government institutions. Digital technology, aligned with incentives of politicians, public administrators, and service providers can be highly effective in improving services. But patronage-based bureaucracies can resist change and e-government advance. These institutional constraints can persist, and cannot be ignored. Sustained collective action is often necessary to address service delivery failures (Chapter 4).

The dividends of digital technology depend on initial institutional conditions and vary by service (World Bank 2016). For services that are easy to monitor and based on routine tasks, digital technologies can improve outcome rapidly, even when institutions are weak, as with cash transfer and licensing. But for services that are hard to monitor and require more discretion from workers, the quality of institutions is more important. In such cases, technology only augments the initial institutional conditions and capabilities, as with teaching, and health services.

A Paradigm Shift in Governance and Public Service

The new ICT tools and platforms are facilitating a power shift in the way citizens engage with the state. The pace of this shift may be uncertain, and perhaps exaggerated for the short term, but the long-term impact is likely to be profound. The rise of social media, the growing number and networking power of civil society organizations (CSOs), mutual learning and information sharing among CSOs, the demographic changes of youth and urban population growth, government decentralization reforms, and open government initiatives and access to public information laws—all are contributing factors for this power shift. These factors are strengthening the demand for good governance and the capability of citizens to hold the state accountable. They are also contributing to the rise of "populism" in politics. ICT complements and reinforces those contributors to the power shift by removing gatekeepers and intermediaries, breaking the monopoly of the state and official channels on news, and helping local NGOs to network and organize. The high costs of ignoring real-time dialogue with citizens should increasingly become evident to governments.

One promising development in the use of ICT by NGOs and CSOs is the training and sharing it enables among NGOs across countries. Social media capacity building is on the rise. While mainstream media has been dominated by the state, it has ignored the youth on which social media focus. Developing countries may enjoy the next wave of democratization and access to information with the explosive growth of their use of mobile and social media.

The call of citizens for government accountability is a testament to the rise of public opinion. Will this reinforce the recent focus on accountability in international development? Since 2005, there have been several international declarations on accountability for aid effectiveness, and a shift from asking that governments in developing countries be accountable to donors to asking them to be directly accountable to their own citizens.[1] For a long time, international development has concentrated on the state,

---

[1] As reflected in the *Paris Declaration on Aid Effectiveness* (2005) and the *Accra Agenda for Action* (2008).

not the full range of institutions that deliver good governance. Are development partners willing to go beyond using *accountability* as a buzzword and to committing whatever it takes in time, resources, political capital, broader engagements, and appropriate organizational cultures?

Taking direct accountability seriously is not without challenges (Odugbemi and Lee 2011). Access to information and ICT is a critical, though not sufficient, condition to this paradigm shift. First, there is the skepticism of technocratic professionals who see accountability measures as political invasions of their comfort zones. Second, there is the tendency to rely on accountability tools—and particularly ICT tools—to do the work, without mobilizing the critical staff and social intermediaries as would be necessary to make the technical tools work. Third, the staff of development agencies face supply-driven incentives and short-time horizons that often get in the way of understanding the local context and the behavior of local stakeholders. Fourth, the tradition of governance reform (the logic of the discipline) has taken a state-centric view of governance, insulating decision-making from democratic control and accountability, and shifting power to technocratic guardians (Odugbemi and Lee 2011; Roberts 2010). This view neglects the roles of citizens (and their intermediaries) and the capacity of those citizens to hold their governments accountable for the governance agenda.

It is hoped that the many examples provided in this book can contribute to our understanding of how to integrate ICT into efforts to enhance the capacity of citizens to hold their governments accountable and to ease some of these challenges. It is also hoped that these examples raise awareness about how initial institutional conditions do shape the impact of digital technologies.

Public Services and Governance Challenges

There is a growing consensus in developing countries that better governance is a key element in promoting growth and inclusive development. Gains in governance across the political, social, and economic spheres have been frustratingly slow. They must be consolidated, sustained, and built upon. Remaining challenges range from strengthening people's confidence in elections, to respect the rule of law, to improve the business environment, and improve accountability for delivery of public services. Corruption remains a major challenge, and it is not limited to government agencies—private sector and NGOs also share significant responsibility.

The global economic and financial environment put further stress on developing countries' governments to deliver basic services, create jobs, ensure global competitiveness, mobilize investment resources, and rely less on external resources of finance for development. There has been marked improvement in economic performance in many developing economies, in Africa, Middle East, and Latin America since the 1990s. But this impressive growth has been driven by a global commodity boom, and has not been matched by structural transformation of the economy.

Such transformation will have to come through diversifying their economies, increasing their shares in global manufacturing, developing their human resources for global competitiveness, developing their infrastructures and logistics, and acquiring capabilities to master the new technologies. These structural transformations depend on improved economic and political governance, transparent and accountable public finance, efficient and responsive delivery of public services, effective and transparent partnership with the private sector, and enabling citizen feedback and participation beyond the electoral cycle. This transformation requires constructive relations between the state and nonstate (citizens, businesses, CSOs)—improving the business and regulatory environment, developing institutions to enforce contracts and property rights, strengthening corporate governance, opening up government data, partnering and engaging with civil society, and collaborating across government agencies to improve public sector governance and performance. In short, country's ability to achieve sustained structural transformation will depend on the political commitment coordination, and cooperation to support capacity building for governance, improve public sector performance, and effect the policy reforms that will enable effective use of the newly built capacity.[2]

Governance and public sector capacity are thus major building blocks of the development strategy of most emerging economies. The governance challenge in Africa and the Middle East is particularly acute, where

---

[2] African governance report, 2016, and previous ones since 2009.

state performance is disappointingly poor, putting further progress on development goals at risk. Results of interventions on the supply side alone have often been disappointing, and therefore strengthening the demand for good governance (DFGG) is a logical and complementary next step. The status of the sociopolitical evolution and economic development of these regions makes the rationale for a more balanced approach between the supply and demand side even more compelling and promising than in perhaps any other region. Political instability and a weak social contract continue to bedevil many countries. Citizens mistrust public institutions and service providers, as many of these institutions remain opaque and fail to deliver on basic services. Weak governance, low public sector capacity, and poor service delivery create a vicious cycle.

Competitiveness is constrained by restrictive business regulations that are difficult to remove because of vested interests. Poor quality of public services is the result of limited capacity, weak incentives, and failures in accountability of civil servants and politicians to the public. Infrastructure development is impeded by poor public investment, budget management, and procurement—and these practices are fed by poor transparency, accountability, and participation.

State performance is disappointingly poor in many parts of the world, putting further progress on development goals at risk. For example, most of Africa's poor are in fragile and conflict-affected countries. Results of interventions on the supply side alone have been disappointing, and so scaling up DFGG is a logical and complementary next step.[3] There is growing consensus that DFGG combined with mobile communications and open government data could be a potential game changer in Africa and globally.

The most critical challenges to realizing the potential of ICTs for public service transformation and governance are political and institutional. These challenges include: shallow understanding of local governance and sociopolitical context; weak enabling policies and institutions;

---

[3] It must be kept in mind, however, that DFGG alone will not lead to sustained improvements in government performance. A virtuous cycle can be created by working simultaneously on supply and demand measures to improve governance and service delivery, as will be discussed later in this book.

weak political commitment; limited capacity of CSOs to scale up and apply public pressure for sustainability; weak partnerships among local stakeholders; and disciplinary blinders and turf barriers among specialists concerned with ICT, governance, social development, and service sectors.

The national ICT ecosystems of many developing countries also present challenges. Recent rapid mobile phone penetration in developing countries far outpaces Internet penetration, and provides an unprecedented opportunity for citizen activism and DFGG. The key challenges are: poor ICT infrastructure; regulatory frameworks and barriers; policies for filtering, censoring, and privacy; textual and numerical illiteracy; underdeveloped local content industry and poorly-maintained government websites; high cost and underdeveloped innovation ecosystem for local developers; and lack of sustainable business models for mobile apps dedicated to social accountability.

The various technologies, approaches, and applications of ICT for governance must be put into a broader context. Experience with deploying ICT for governance shows the crucial importance of understanding the social, political, institutional, informational, and stakeholder contexts for ICT and DFGG interventions. Both providers and consumers of services can benefit from information flows that enable consumers to exercise influence on the quality of service, while providers can offer better services when they can obtain timely inputs on their performance, provided incentives are aligned with this objective. A range of state and nonstate actors can be involved in strengthening DFGG, as DFGG initiatives genuinely gather momentum when they are built around a reform coalition. Research also shows how context shapes technological impact: we must avoid a deterministic view of technology. This calls for understanding the incentives, capabilities, and strategies of the stakeholders, and the institutional and sociopolitical contexts within which a technological intervention is meant to increase accountability.

Aims and Structure of the Book

My aim is to raise awareness about the potential and current state of digital technologies (i.e., ICT) as a means to transform public services and enhance government accountability and civic participation in governance across developing countries. The book highlights the importance of the policies and institutions that might sustain and scale up ICT for governance and public service improvement. It points to the opportunities ICT offers to transform government institutions to become open, transparent, responsive, and accountable. It also points to the challenges and constraints to pursuing such a transformation. It suggests that digital technologies are helping to share information, expand knowledge and improve interactions among stakeholders, but they have not democratized knowledge or overcome the educational, economic, or social divides, or the highly unequal complementary assets and capabilities to turn information into useful knowledge and power. In doing so, the book provides a basis for policy dialogue within governments and with service providers, development partners, and CSOs seeking to create enabling environments for responsive service delivery and good governance.

The book is divided into five chapters. The first chapter provides an overview of the opportunities and challenges of harnessing digital technologies for transforming public services and strengthening governance. The second chapter identifies the broad categories of digital technologies and illustrates their role in strengthening social accountability and DFGG. The third chapter discusses the concepts and technologies already introduced to public service and governance functions such as resource management and public service delivery. It surveys the opportunities for service innovation and governance and how to realize them. The fourth chapter identifies the political, institutional, and ICT ecosystem challenges facing developing nations. The final chapter draws conclusions and recommendations for exploiting the vast potential of digital technologies, while taking account of the contextual factors and challenges facing governance in developing countries. This concluding chapter offers guidelines for policy makers, development professionals, and service providers: understand the context and motivations of stakeholders, balance short- and long-term objectives to improve public services and accountability, seek partnerships and build capacity, synergistically deploy supply and demand measures, strategically select entry points for interventions, integrate pro-poor policies into ICT for public service innovation and governance, and learn fast from experience.

CHAPTER 2

Technologies and Approaches

In this chapter, we focus on the key technologies, platforms, and approaches that can be harnessed for good governance, even while recognizing the limits and pitfalls:

- We first outline the expanding array of tools and platforms that can enhance governance; public service delivery improvement and citizen-complaint resolution; citizen-engagement and real-time analytics; malaria prevention tracking; crisis reporting; participatory planning and budgeting; and participatory regulation, among others.
- Second, as part of this expanding array, we explore the potential of mobile activism.
- Third, we show how access to mobile phones, smartphones, wireless connectivity, and broadband is being complemented by key enablers to the effective use of this access: social media, digital platforms, Digital Identification, and open data.
- Fourth, we examine the role of crowdsourcing and open innovation in enhancing governance, collaboration, and open services innovation.
- Fifth, we look at the role of open government in leveraging the data sharing revolution and spurring participation, transparency, and innovation within government, and among business, civil society organizations (CSOs), and citizens.
- We end the chapter with a broad assessment of the promises, limits and potential risks of digital technologies.

An Expanding Array of Technologies

New information technologies are sweeping the planet, with profound implications for public service accountability and governance. They have the potential to transform the process by which state and nonstate actors interact to develop and implement policies and services, and thus transform the development process. The aim is to raise the awareness of policy makers and service providers about the versatility of these technologies and the vast opportunities they promise to open. Chapter 3 will further illustrate how ICT can strengthen the supply of government services and functions and, at the same time, also strengthen the demand for good governance and social accountability.

The Internet and mobile phones have become ubiquitous platforms for communications and developmental applications that engage citizens and enhance the transparency and accountability of public services. Such technological interventions aim to improve service and product responsiveness (and by extension to hold to account the public agencies and corporations responsible for those services and products). Similarly, mass users tend to be more often the primary users of information for service and product accountability interventions. The range of applications is fast expanding and many innovations come from developing countries, particularly those who leapfrogged to mobile communications. Here are a few examples:

Kiirti (Bangalore, India, http://www.kiirti.org/) is a platform that aims to facilitate complaint resolution from citizens. As such, NGOs can adapt Kiirti to their specific needs and use it in place of technological capabilities they lack. Kiirti is SMS enabled and has established web-based and digitized phone reporting. The platform receives information from mass individual users, which is verified by the NGO using it. Once the information is verified, the NGO works with the necessary government officials to resolve any given problems and then report back to the citizens affected.

Cidade Democrática (Brazil, http://www.cidadedemocratica.com.br/) is a collaborative action platform that enables citizens, organizations, and governmental institutions to report problems and propose solutions related to matters of concern in Brazilian cities. The idea underlying

Cidade Democratica is that citizens should assume responsibility over their streets, neighborhoods, and cities, and thus take an active part in local problem solving and promoting political causes. The platform covers a wide range of municipal issues, from environment and health to transport, education, and planning. Cidade Democratica receives information from mass users—including residents and clients of public services—and from NGOs that aim to solve some problem in their urban environment. NGOs and individual users may then use the information to promote their social and political causes. Journalists, opinion leaders, and politicians also use the information posted on Cidade Democratica for their work.

EpiSurveyor (Guatemala) is a mobile-phone-based application used to conduct national surveys. It was used to survey the beneficiaries of Mi Familia Progresa (Mifapro), Guatemala's conditional cash-transfer program, aiming to fight poverty. While Mifapro has the potential to significantly reduce extreme poverty, its main challenges lie in the effective management of its monitoring and evaluation system, including its monitoring of conditionalities in health and education. A critical step toward overcoming this challenge is to gain access to quick and accurate firsthand information on activities at rural clinics and schools in isolated parts of the country. This puts a premium on a cost-effective mechanism to collect field data and survey program beneficiaries.

mGesa (Kenya) uses mobile and interactive mapping to promote children's health and education, with the help of Plan International. It aims to enhance georeferenced information in support of program design, monitoring, and evaluation, and to improve the accessibility of updated maps and data for broader participation. It deploys needs-driven geographic information system GIS) (*PoiMapper*) for mobile phones and personal computers. Geodata come from multiple sources, and are integrated with open-source GIS tools. Early feedback from users indicates that visual display of georeferenced data can help decision-making. It is also affordable, easy to use, and can be customized and integrated with basic mobile-phone functionalities. *PoiMapper* is being used in many other applications: humanitarian mapping and rapid situational assessments for crisis and relief work, farmland and forestry mapping for participation and monitoring in agriculture and rural development planning, as well as for environment and climate change monitoring.

Digitally enabled agricultural extension services can play a key role in bridging the information gap to enable women—the main contributors to the agricultural sector in developing countries—to improve their productivity. Women and rural communities are able to access information on improving the quality of their products, acquiring improved seeds and crop varieties, accessing materials and equipment, controlling disease and pest, conserving soil, and developing production skills.

For example, in Uganda, the *Enhancing Access to Agricultural Information* project, implemented by the Women of Uganda Network in partnership with the Technical Centre for Agriculture, has improved the livelihoods of women through providing relevant agricultural information to farmers. Women farmers' questions on agricultural and other topics—such as goat rearing, bean agronomy, and poultry keeping—are discussed on weekly radio talk shows. Relevant agricultural information is sourced or produced, repackaged into local content, and disseminated via radio and SMS as well as on audiotapes, video tapes, and CD-ROMs. The content is made available in the local language.

RapidSMS (Nigeria) is transforming the way data can be collected and utilized, using a free and open-source framework for dynamic data collection, logistics coordination, and communication, leveraging SMS mobile-phone technology, and enabling governments and organizations to more effectively manage the delivery of projects and services. It seeks to open access to a large volume of accurate, timely, and actionable information at low cost in areas related to public service delivery, distribution, and logistics.

RapidSMS was applied to malaria containment in Nigeria. The challenge was how to best distribute long-lasting insecticide-treated nets to prevent deaths caused by Malaria. This required effective tracking, monitoring, and reporting from the communities, and getting quick responses for efficient and effective distribution during the planned campaigns. A website was developed and made available for stakeholders to monitor the campaign in real time, coordinate field activities, and analyze data. The more effective distribution of the nets had a significant impact on malaria prevention, which is particularly crucial in Nigeria where malaria is responsible for about 66 percent of all clinic visits and deaths of 250,000 children every year (World Bank).

Despite the many promising pilots and innovations in leveraging mobile applications to foster service innovation and governance, it is too early for the full potential of mobile to be realized in developing countries. Mobile phones can support various methods of activism with relatively little financial means compared to earlier times and other more complex digital technologies. Several free and open-source software tools are already available to extend the basic features of mobile phones. Potential growth will depend as much on the political space given to activist NGOs, activist networks, and other participants in the political process as on technological advances.

Five Potential Trends for Mobile Activism

Mobile participation through citizen media. One example is a project called *Voices of Africa*, in which mobile reporters across Africa use mobile phones to report on events and also send video interviews that are then published on the Internet. Mobile phones can also be used to produce content later delivered by traditional media, such as *SW Radio Africa.*

Local innovation in mobile tools and activism. According to a study by the United Nations Foundation, key benefits of mobile technology for all NGOs include time savings (95 percent) as well as the ability to quickly mobilize and organize individuals (91 percent), reach audiences that were previously difficult or impossible to reach (74 percent), transmit data more quickly and accurately (67 percent), and gather data more quickly and accurately (59 percent). It is up to the creativity of activists as to how they will use the mobile phone as an instrument to coordinate protests, mobilize campaigns, and raise funds.

Using the mobile phone as a tool for monitoring transparency and data collection. Advances in this area include building open information repositories through the participation of mobile users, establishing citizen monitoring systems to act as watchdogs, and using advanced mobile features for analysis and independent research results. Mobile phones now offer high access and mobility along with a ubiquitous platform for easy-to-develop applications for collecting data and monitoring and reporting on events. Mobile phones are becoming powerful tools for timely and accurate data collection. When combined with global positioning system (GPS) capabilities, mobile phones can improve the utility of such data. Recognizing and harnessing this potential can provide high returns for future survey exercises and, as such, strengthen public service and program management in a quick and cost-effective manner.

Using mobile phones for advocacy and to mobilize activists across a country. This not only involves using mobile phones to collect data, but also helps disseminate results for advocacy. The Collecting and Exchange of Local Agricultural Content project in Uganda is an example of how such efforts can be applied to the local context. Farmers can document their knowledge about cultivation practices on different media, made available in a local repository.

Using mobile phones to help network, coordinate, and mobilize around causes. Besides Facebook and Twitter, another example of a highly successful social network application is *MXit* (http://mxit.com) from South Africa, a free instant-messaging software application that runs on 3G mobile phones. *MXit* is mainly used by young people and acts as a chat room, but its messages are cheaper than regular SMS. One project in South Africa uses *MXit* for counseling services, where young people can address burning questions on topics such as violence or sexuality and receive answers. Although it is a chat tool, it shows the potential for peer-to-peer networking, through which activists everywhere can be connected with one another. *MXit* could create networks built around causes such as public services.

The Enablers

Access to mobile, smart phones, wireless connectivity, and broadband is being complemented by a wide array of enablers of effective use of this access. Of particular importance are three broad enablers: social media, digital platforms (including digital ID), and open data.

Social media. Social media platforms are diffusing quickly across the world. They are credited with many economic dividends, including encouraging political mobilization and social change, spreading democratic ideas, facilitating citizen participation, and reducing the transaction costs for all kinds of economic and financial transactions. However, much is still to be learned about the role of social media in promoting governance and innovation in public services, and in operating in different social and political contexts. Much to learn is also needed about avoiding the dark side of social media: inciting terrorism, violence and bullying, political manipulation (fake news, and loss of privacy, and so on, What is however clear is that the youth of developing countries have taken to the adoption of social media as a major platform for information and interaction.

Digital platforms. These are digital mediums that allow people to connect to it for all kinds of transactions and applications, such as digital payments, mobile money service (e.g., M-Pesa), e-commerce platforms (e.g., Amazon, e-Bay, Ali Baba), Facebook, Twitter, and so on.

Digital identification platforms (biometric or unique ID). Lack of personal official identification (ID) hinders people from exercising their rights and isolates them economically and socially. Voting, receipt of social benefits and public services, and use of financial services are off limits. Robust digital ID systems can produce significant savings for citizens and government, and enable digital delivery of public and business services. Pakistan used digital ID to facilitate social benefits to poor women and emergency relief.

Digital ID systems also advance government transparency and accountability, and reduce corruption. A 2010 biometric consensus of civil servants in Guinea-Bissau reportedly identified 4,000 nonexistent workers on the public payroll. Nigeria reported eliminating 43,000 "ghost" workers in the first phase of a pilot in 2011 that saved $67 million. In Botswana, biometric enrollment of pension and social grants eliminated waste by identifying duplicate records and deceased beneficiaries.[1]

Programs to develop digital ID systems aim to "make everyone count" by providing a unique identity and delivering digital ID-enabled services to all. Trust in data security will be critical to wide adoption and use of digital ID across all sectors.

Open data. Data are growing exponentially, thanks to digitization of all kinds of processes and data collection, GPS, and mobile. Open data come primarily from government and promise many economic and social

---

[1] http://www.worldbank.org/transport/connections (April 2015).

dividends. Yet, public agencies are reluctant to share data, particularly on their performance and expenditures, and unwilling to expose their data to scrutiny. More on this later.

Crowdsourcing and Open Service Innovation

Crowdsourcing is a distributed problem-solving and coproduction model. In the classic use of the term, problems are broadcast to an unknown group of solvers in the form of an open call for solutions. The difference between crowdsourcing and ordinary outsourcing is that in crowdsourcing a task or problem is outsourced to an undefined public rather than a specific body.

Users typically form online communities, and the crowd submits solutions. The crowd also sorts through the solutions, finding the best ones. The best solutions are then owned by the entity that broadcast the problem in the first place—the crowdsourcer—and the winning individuals in the crowd are sometimes rewarded. In some cases, this labor is well compensated, either monetarily, with prizes, or with recognition. In other cases, the only rewards may be recognition or intellectual satisfaction.

With the increase of web applications' capabilities over the past two decades, the possibilities for crowdsourcing techniques have greatly increased, and now the term often refers exclusively to web-based activity. While the potential for web-based crowdsourcing has existed for many years, it has not been well implemented until recently.

Perceived benefits of crowdsourcing include the following:

- Problems can be explored at comparatively little cost, and often very quickly.
- Payment is optional.
- The organization can tap a wider range of talent than might be present in its own organization.
- By listening to the crowd, organizations gain firsthand insight into their customers' desires.
- The community may feel a brand-building kinship with the crowdsourcing organization, which is the result of an earned sense of ownership through contribution and collaboration.

Crowdsourcing also has the potential to be a problem-solving mechanism for government and nonprofit use. Urban and transit planning are prime areas for crowdsourcing. One early application to test crowdsourcing was the 2008–2009 public participation process for transit planning in Salt Lake City, Utah, funded by a U.S. Federal Transit Administration grant. Another notable application of crowdsourcing to government problem solving is the Peer to Patent Community Patent Review project for the U.S. Patent and Trademark Office. More recently, several U.S. Federal agencies have begun to use crowdsourcing platforms to seek solutions to both major and minor public challenges, and to draw lessons for best practices in using crowdsourcing as a tool for improving services and coinnovating with the public.

The practice of crowdsourcing is emerging in developing countries, mainly in the private sector and civil society. Locally developed platforms, such as Ushahidi, have offered an open coworking and community space for crowdsourcing innovation, and the formation of new companies. New crowdsourcing and communication channels such as Ushahidi also enable an entire emergency ecosystem to operate like a coherent entity. A new paradigm for humanitarian effort is emerging, where victims and social intermediaries supply on-the-ground data (during and immediately after a crisis) using mobile phones or whatever channels available to them. Self-organized volunteers and intermediaries triage this data, authenticate text messages, and plot incidents on interactive mapping displays that help aid workers target their response. Crisis-mapping communities have emerged and rallied together in a matter of days in response to crises ranging from the earthquake in Haiti, wild fires in Russia, exposure to radiation in Japan, medicine shortages in Africa, to elections in Kenya and India.

A new type of crowdsourcing is a collaborative or cooperative effort to solve problems and innovate solutions that use competition as a motivator for participation or performance. Crowdsourcing for open innovation and collaborative problem solving is spreading rapidly in the business sector. Governments in the United States and some other industrialized countries have begun to use crowdsourcing to organize contests for citizens and small businesses to develop innovative solutions to public services and public goods, with encouraging results. In principle, the use of crowdsourcing for innovation by governments, in collaboration with their citizens or clients, can be a major source of service improvement and citizen engagement in developing countries.

GlobalGiving and Amplifying Local Voices

Another variation of crowdsourcing is **crowdfunding platforms (e.g., kickstarter), to mobilize sums of money from many small contributors and fans for a cause such as disaster recovery, or social software application. One example is** to use such platforms to capture narratives from a large number of beneficiaries from the field and turn their stories into data, which can then be used for analysis and quick feedback (Stanford Social Innovation Review 2011). GlobalGiving (http://www.globalgiving.org) matches a large number of donors with the needs of a large number of small grantees (NGOs with projects and needs to be met). It has begun to use "Sense Maker" software that enables people to put their stories into context and then turns this raw information into data that can be visually represented and analyzed around topics. The GlobalGiving online platform is being updated with maps to show the locations along with narrative feedback on each project.

GlobalGiving is using this ICT application to accelerate story gathering from the field, to assess feedback, and to mobilize and allocate resources quickly based on voices from the field. This is likely to lead to much faster detection of successes and failures, thus driving down the cost of evaluation. It should make the process of matching donors with projects more effective for development and poverty alleviation.

Open Government Data

Half a century ago, no country had laws specifically requiring government officials to provide information to their citizens. Today, about 80 countries do, and the number is still growing. Governments are being pressed to go beyond "freedom of information" acts to openly sharing their data with the public (open data, readable and readily manipulated by ICT tools), and, more recently, to proactively foster the creative use of government data through open government initiatives.

With the increasing digitization of government processes, the amount of rich and valuable data has increased not only for officials, but also for the public as a whole. If made available in a user-friendly and interoperable format, government data can unlock a wealth of insight, promote industry and social innovation, and engage citizens in governance, service improvement, and socioeconomic development.

The U.S. Federal Government, for example, is now asking how the data revolution can be leveraged to spur participation, transparency, and innovation across businesses and citizens. The government started an Open Government Initiative in late 2009, with the beginning of a new administration. It outlined major steps: publishing government information online, improving the quality of information, institutionalizing a culture of openness, and creating an enabling policy framework. Since then, the sheer volume of data now available to citizens is unprecedented. The government also provides analytical tools to set the data free and help users make data available for their needs.[2]

The theory behind open data is that by improving the citizen's access to public data, citizen-led government accountability will increase. Data empowers; metrics matter. But open data do not guarantee open government. Open government implies changes in the culture of government and how it relates to citizens as clients. Such changes require pressure from civil society, cooperation from civil servants, and commitment from political leaders and policy makers. Government agencies have to learn to listen more effectively to their citizens, and citizens need to learn to better "consume" data.

Putting the data out before the public eye is not enough, particularly in developing countries and poor communities. Relevant processes and social intermediaries must be in place to expand people's information capabilities and to help them make use of such data for participation, innovation, and accountability. Fluency in using data might become a form of basic literacy. A more likely scenario for developing countries is for local social intermediaries to play a key role in interpreting data,

---

[2] The U.S. Open Government Initiative is still in the early stages of implementation, its immediate benefits are still to be proven, and its budget was cut in early 2011 as part of the government's austerity measures. Nevertheless, the initiative has generated many lessons and high expectations and many countries are following suite.

applying analytics and interactive mapping, and using the data to press for more openness, transparency, accountability. This would initiate and sustain a virtuous cycle. Empowered citizens would lead to more open government, and vice versa.

Small-scale experimentation or "learning by doing" can be used to gradually change the culture and build the capacity of governments to sustain openness and collaboration. Openly engaging with citizens and social intermediaries is a new experience for civil servants the world over, and particularly in developing countries. Such transformation requires the ability and incentives to listen to citizens and to increase understanding of client needs and behavior. Sustainable initiatives of open government also require preparing public agencies to respond to feedback, while strengthening citizen demand for more information and engagement.

An IBM study (Lee and Kwak 2011) of several open government initiatives in several U.S. agencies has concluded that government agencies could follow a phased approach to implementation (Box 2.1). This approach would start with identifying high-priority data and improving the quality and availability of such data using conventional web applications. In the second stage, agencies would welcome and utilize inputs from the public and apply social media and Web 2.0 such as blogs, social networking, and ideation tools to online public forums. In the third stage, agencies would enhance open collaboration with the public and private sector by sharing government data and feedback through collaborative applications to cocreate services. Finally, agencies would expand their portfolio of open-source initiatives to realize ubiquitous engagement, leveraging mobile computing and seamlessly engaging the public across government.

This study offers some guidelines for effective data sharing, stressing the need for prioritizing, piloting, and learning. Public leaders and development practitioners should be cognizant of the need to prepare government agencies to be able to respond to the demands of open government and DFGG and service improvement. Adequate preparation on the supply and demand side can help create a virtuous cycle for public service improvement, innovation, and accountability. Depending on context and political commitment, leapfrogging some stages may be possible. But this option also carries substantial risks, particularly where resources are scarce and institutional capabilities for supply responses weak.

Box 2.1

Open Government, Implemented in Stages

One approach to implementing open government recommends that government agencies advance their open government initiatives incrementally, in four stages, focusing on one implementation stage at a time. Starting from increasing data transparency (stage one), the process moves on to improving open participation (stage two), enhancing open collaboration (stage three), and realizing ubiquitous engagement (stage four). Following this sequence, agencies can minimize risks and effectively harness the power of social media to engage the public.

Stage One: Increasing Data Transparency

Agencies at this stage focus on increasing transparency of government processes and performance by publishing relevant data online and sharing it with the public. The two most important tasks in this stage are:

- Identifying high-value, high-impact data for the public
- Improving and assuring data quality in terms of accuracy, consistency, and timeliness

Social media is not deployed at this stage because conventional Web applications provide adequate capabilities for increasing data transparency.

Stage Two: Improving Open Participation

Agencies at this stage focus on improving open participation of the public in government work and decision making through various methods and tools. Open participation enhances policy decisions and government services by welcoming and utilizing the input of the public. In stage two, agencies use social media and Web 2.0 tools, including Web dialogues, blogs, microblogging, social networking, photo/video sharing, social bookmarking/tagging, and ideation tools, to create online public forums for engaging in anecdotes, stories, conversations, ideas, and comments.

Stage Three: Enhancing Open Collaboration

Agencies at this stage strive to collaborate not only with other agencies but also with the public and the private sector by sharing government data and public inputs and feedback. Open collaboration refers to public engagement in complex tasks or projects that aim to produce specific outputs and cocreate value-added services. Open collaboration applications include group writing and editing of documents, wiki applications development, open-source software development, organizing events, policy/rule making, public response to national emergencies/natural disasters, and innovation of products and services. Collaboration relies on collaborative social media such as wikis, Google docs, and Jive SBS.

Stage Four: Realizing Ubiquitous Engagement

Agencies at this stage take transparency, participation, and collaboration to the next level of public engagement. The agencies improve and fine-tune existing open government initiatives to maximize their benefits. Furthermore, they expand their portfolio of open government initiatives to further benefit the public. Agencies strive to achieve two important goals: first, ubiquitous mobile computing devices facilitate public engagement; and second, various public engagement methods, tools, and services are seamlessly integrated within and across government agencies so that the public can easily engage in various activities without having to log in and out of different applications.

To effectively implement their open government initiatives, the study recommends that governments:

- Use a phased implementation approach
- Use a democratic, bottom-up approach
- Consider conducting pilot projects and/or establishing centers for excellence
- Secure necessary resources
- Prioritize the use of the 80/20 rule
- Align open government initiatives with the agency's goals

- Establish governance mechanisms for data sharing
- Expand the number of metrics over time
- Address cultural barriers
- Make public engagement an everyday routine
- Institutionalize incentives
- Establish enterprise architecture early in the process
- Integrate public engagement application
- Develop communities of practice across government
- Develop and communicate a government-wide strategy

Source: Lee and Kwak 2011.

The U.K. government issued an Open Public Service White Paper that put open government data within a comprehensive policy framework for all public services (U.K. Minister of Government Policy 2011). The vision is to set a reform process that follows a set of guiding principles to place power for service improvement in the hands of citizens and frontline staff, with additional incentives to help boost those who would otherwise be disadvantaged in the marketplace. Five principles are set to modernize public services:

- Wherever possible increase choice by giving people (or their locally elected representatives) direct control over the services they use.
- Decentralize public services to the lowest appropriate level.
- Open public services to a range of providers (high-quality service can be provided by the public sector, voluntary and community sector, private sector, or through partnerships).
- Ensure fair access to public services (without intervention in new markets, there is the risk of exacerbating current inequalities).
- Make public services responsive and accountable to users and taxpayers (as information about services becomes more transparent, people should be able to make informed choices about the providers they use, voice their opinions, and exercise their democratic rights; meanwhile, elected representatives should be able to scrutinize providers more effectively).

These principles—choice, decentralization, diversity, fairness, and accountability—should guide the detailed reform and innovation of services. Their implementation will require consulting and engaging users as well as current and potential providers of services about the best way to realize these principles. Any government must pace its reforms to ensure it balances the public's need for change with the capacity of public service providers to deliver that change.

ICT has opened up many opportunities to change public service delivery. Yet it is the broader aims of public sector reform that must guide ICT use (not the other way around) to achieve holistic change, scale, and sustainability.

The "Opening Government" Movement

How can we relate the models and experiences of the frontrunners in open data and open government in industrialized countries to the conditions of developing countries? One promising initiative is the "opening government" movement.

In 2011 a small group of government and civil society leaders from around the world gathered to brainstorm how to build upon growing global momentum around transparency, accountability, and civic participation in governance and public service improvement. The result was the creation of the Open Government Partnership (OGP), a new, multistakeholder coalition of government, civil society, and private sector actors working to advance open government around the world—with the goals of increasing public sector responsiveness to citizens, countering corruption, promoting economic efficiencies, harnessing innovation, and improving the delivery of services. In September 2011 the founding OGP governments gathered on the margins of the UN General Assembly to embrace a set of high-level open government principles, announce country-specific commitments for putting these principles into practice, and invite civil society to assess their performance going forward (Open Society Foundation 2011).

To help government, civil society, and private sector actors plan their OGP commitments, the Transparency and Accountability Initiative has gathered current best practices and practical steps to share with OGP participants and other governments. The result was the first document of its kind to compile state-of-the-art efforts toward transparency, accountability, and citizen participation across 15 areas of governance, ranging from broad categories such as access to information, service delivery, and budgeting to specific sectors.

A key area of the OGP is encouraging open government data. Best practices include proactive disclosure of existing digital data on the web, the creation of a negative list of information that may not be shared so that all other information can be made publically available immediately, and the setting of a timeline to ensure that proactive disclosure of government records and other information occurs on a regular basis. More advanced and ambitious steps in the move toward open government data are also recommended (Box 2.2).

The open government data movement is catching up—even in low-income countries—to capture moments of transformational political change. On July 8, 2011, President Mwai Kibaki launched the Kenyan Open Data Initiative (http://opendata.go.ke), making key government data freely available to the public through a single online portal. The census data, national and regional expenditures, and information on key public services were among the first data sets to be released. Tools and applications were built to take these data and make them more useful than they originally were. Kenya provides an early example from developing countries, where the open data ecosystem is still maturing.

The Promises and Limits of Technology

Access to information and a communication infrastructure are key prerequisites for effective accountability, and ICT has the potential to provide these prerequisites in ways that can be superior to the traditional media. Access to information is fundamental. Without information citizens cannot know their eligibility for services, the status of these services, other people's experiences with them, how to get them, which political factions work toward citizen's needs, and so on. The mere delivery of services without accountability is not sufficient to achieve good governance or sustained improvement in service delivery.

Box 2.2

Advanced Steps to Open Government Data

Once the initial steps of providing access to existing digital government data are made, the goal is for all government data to be made available in a form that ensures ease of use and reuse. All information released requires a proper underpinning in informational policy and technological support to realize full transparency, citizen participation, and full social and economic value. Governments should use smarter technologies to ensure that the policy commitment to open government data can be realized in practice. In particular, system searchability greatly helps to ensure access.

Policy and Process Recommendations Include:

- Formulation of an information policy that deals comprehensively with best practices in information collection, storage, retrieval, and management at the national level, and allows for the adoption of the policy either with modification or directly by subnational governments; part of this policy must ensure that most new information is either created in a digital form or is digitized from paper as soon as practicable.
- Formulation of a technological policy that mandates the use of open standards in all e-governance to promote interoperability and prevent vendor lock-in, with only temporary and limited exceptions. This must be accompanied by a document on the e-governance interoperability framework policy, and a national enterprise architecture that lays down the broad parameters of the technology framework to enable efficient information architecture, including metadata standards. The ability to reuse published data must be guaranteed as part of a public sector information/ open government data policy. This is crucial to enable access for journalists, civil society organizations, and others.
- Finally, all information must be provided free of cost, at least in cases where the government isn't monetizing the data, nor has plans to do so, or the data are for use by individuals and small and medium enterprises (SMEs), or the data are available

without any special fees under right to information/freedom of information statutes.

Ambitious steps are also needed to ensure that open government data reach the public. Public outreach and citizen-oriented tools are crucial to ensuring a vibrant public sphere—both online and offline—where government data are used and discussed and a feedback loop is created, rather than a data dump. Using service-oriented architecture will help ensure platform independence, better scalability, greater code reuse, higher availability of services, the parallel development of different components, and many other benefits in terms of provision of data for governments. A robust service-oriented architecture will enable citizens to be treated as yet another client requesting information, and will enable useful application programming interfaces (APIs) to be built that will allow for easy access to the data.

Under the most ambitious regime, social media integration is a must, because it allows governments to leverage network effects and defray costs. Such integration will allow governments to go where the citizens are rather than trying to get the citizens to come to them. But care must be taken to ensure that such integration is done with adequate safeguards for privacy, and long-term archival and data portability.

Policy and process recommendations include: (i) neutralizing the proelite bias that is often inherent in online technologies to ensure that there is no elitist capture of the benefits of open government data, and that there is active promotion of "offline translation" of data, especially in technologically divided countries where the gap is wide; (ii) allowing for correction of data by the public; and (iii) facilitating offline translation of data, especially in technologically poorer countries.

These recommendations require that multiple forms of access must be provided to the data. The data must be made available interactively through the Web for nontechnical users. For more advanced users of the data, the data must be available for bulk data downloads. There also should be a single-point portal (such as Data.gov) to provide access to different public authorities' data. Finally, all data should be cloud based to the extent that it lowers government overhead.

Source: Author, summarized from Transparency and Accountability Initiative 2011.

Radio is the one traditional mass medium that has the widest reach in developing countries, and in terms of technical reach, outperforms any new ICT. In democracies, campaigns strongly rely on the mass media, and, most recently, new media technologies. In autocratic states, where several factors hinder the mass media from providing avenues for accountability, ICT may to some degree overcome these factors. The traditional media in developing countries face economic and political pressures in supporting accountability, as they are privately financed or government controlled. In many countries, strong political players own large parts of the media, providing a powerful channel for transmitting their convictions. These dangers are less relevant for ICT, particularly the Internet and mobile phones.

The traditional media mostly provide a one-way communications channel, with limited openings for citizen feedback. ICT not only allows for two-way information flows and a wide range of communication channels and forums that citizens can use, but also magnifies their voices and allows them to be anonymous. Costs for mobilizing citizens through mobile phones and the Internet are relatively low since users' physical presence is not required, economic costs to individuals are marginal, and political risks can be minimized through anonymity.[3]

ICT also provides the infrastructure for a public forum that brings together the diverse viewpoints that can serve as the basis for informed public deliberation. This is particularly critical in postconflict states and deeply divided societies, as a way of encouraging dialogue and interaction. Market-based media make it difficult to be heard. Compared to TV and newspapers, radio has low technical and editorial barriers, allowing citizens to use it to make their voices heard.

Technical convergence is allowing the merging of infrastructures such as mobile phones, radio, television, and satellite and the possibility of providing the same content on different platforms. Accountability and citizen feedback need multiple platforms, and information needs to be provided through all relevant channels. ICT, in combination with traditional media, provides opportunities for a wider and

---

[3] ICT can also magnify voices of subversives and those not supportive of democracy.

more targeted reach, even in the poorest countries. Creating community multimedia centers combines both traditional and new ICT tools to reach the broadest audience possible and to tailor content to targeted audiences.

To help transparency and accountability, ICT can be used as a tool to:

- Process, disclose, and disseminate information (that is, as an information and transparency tool)—supply-side activities for accountability for service delivery.
- Campaign for accountability and encourage participation (that is, as an inclusive, participatory tool for monitoring and oversight as well as capacity building).
- Network social intermediaries, enable their upward and downward accountabilities, and enhance their mobilization efforts.
- Organize information, for example, by providing a one-stop online data gateway that organizes information relevant to specific accountability issues.
- Mash and blend information from various sources—for example, social, economic, and spatial data from geomapping or from traditional broadcasting and social media.
- Visualize information and make it accessible to citizens, for example, by compiling data on development activities into animated graphs and other easily understood formats.
- Support communities of practice in different areas of accountability, For example, the WOUGNET, combines online platforms, offline workshops, and mobile-phone applications and is a common platform to share information, network, provide technical support to women, and advocate for gender issues (Arnold 2011).

The potential of mobile communication technology involves four elements that together create a virtuous cycle of innovation that can benefit all citizens: (i) access—innovations in ICT are steadily expanding the mobile "footprint" to cover a larger percentage of the population; (ii) affordability, due to the combination of prepaid service plans and cheaper mobile handsets; (iii) appliance innovation—making these devices more adaptable to a growing range of needs and services relevant to all citizens; and (iv) applications—there has been a vast increase in a few years in the development and rollout of mobile applications. Under certain conditions, these virtuous cycles can lead to increased participation, and more transparent, accountable, and responsive governance, and where citizens see public services as their right and not as favors.

Digital technologies may fail to empower citizens, however. ICT for government and public service improvement requires effective leadership to make the necessary changes in government rules and management practices, to overcome resistance to change from vested interests, and to respond to citizen feedback. All this requires a willing government. The promise of digital technologies is that it can encourage good leadership by empowering citizens to hold policy makers and service providers accountable via free and fair elections, more informed voting, more informed service users, and mobilized citizen voice and collective action. Emerging evidence suggests that digital technologies have made elections freer and fairer by improving voter registration and reducing errors in voting, and by better monitoring to curb electoral fraud and violence. Digital technologies, particularly social media, have galvanized citizen protests. But except where governments are willing and able, they have not sustained collective action and citizen voice to improve service delivery. In the hands of repressive regimes, ICT also poses significant risks. Governments can use ICT to monitor and persecute dissenters, filter and censor the Internet, and disseminate false news, thus further undermine personal privacy and human rights. In short, the Internet and other digital technologies could become a tool of control, not a tool of expanding freedom, a shining light on corruption, or a window on the world.

Over time, governments, CSOs, and citizens are learning both the potential and limits or risks of digital technologies for governance, and the ingredients for accountability and participatory democracy. So far, the record in developing countries has been mixed. Digital channels for mobilizing and empowering citizens to pressure policy makers and make them responsive proved effective in democratic countries. But they have not been as effective in initiating and sustaining reforms and in pressing unwilling governments to be more accountable. While these "tools of freedom" can be used to promote democracy and accountability, the outcome is not preordained, even in democratic societies. It will depend on complementary changes in political economy and institutions, sustained by active and informed citizens. It may take a while to succeed in overcoming decades of authoritarianism and extractive institutions. This record, however, is rather short. It is likely that this record will improve with the wide diffusion and multiplications of these channels and with the growing capabilities of CSOs to use these channels. As the communications landscape gets denser and more participatory, the networked population should gain greater access to information, more opportunities to engage in public conversation and speech, and a vastly enhanced ability to organize and undertake public action.

Preparing for Emerging Technologies

The promise of emerging technologies is even much greater than the potential and demonstrated impact of widely available digital technologies. These emerging technologies may include artificial intelligence and machine learning, fifth generation (5G) mobile broadband, Internet of Things (IoT), connecting devices, Blockchain,[4] quantum computing, and the sharing or circular economy[5] (turning consumers into coproducers/cocreators), among others. They have the potential to overcome key limitations of existing ICTs, increase access to ultra-high speed communication and computing, at much lower costs, enable smarter ways of collaborating and coproducing, turn physical assets into shared services, and/or deliver new, more inclusive, personalized and high-quality services. Many of these are not futuristic technologies even for developing countries. For example, China plans to begin 5G trials in 10 cities and aims to commercialize the technology by 2018. Similarly, in India telecom companies are in talks with Nokia for 5G trials.

---

[4] See, for example, https://www.ted.com/talks/don_tapscott_how_the_blockchain_is_changing_money_and_business

[5] https://www.youtube.com/watch?v=Cd_isKtGaf8

As advances in ICT continue to accelerate, the challenge for all countries will be in preparing themselves to master the new technological capabilities and associated practices. Increasingly, the binding constraints to realizing ICT potential will be nontechnical: transformative leadership, enabling policies and institutions, augmenting change management capabilities, nurturing relevant applications and local content, promoting widespread literacy, and sustaining a vibrant governance ecosystem.

CHAPTER 3

Opportunities for Service Innovation and Governance

In this chapter we identify where ICT may be applied to enhance innovation and governance in public services and the participation of citizens in the continuous improvement of these services:

- First, we provide an overview of how ICT broadens the opportunities for citizens to participate, access information on government performance, and hold the state accountable.
- Second, using many examples, we outline a conceptual framework that links both supply and demand for good governance and public services improvement. Technology applications for government and governance are categorized in terms of key functions rather than specific agencies, technologies, or techniques. These functions include: resource management, service delivery to citizens, regulation and services to business, and political oversight and participation.
- Third, we show how various technologies could be used as powerful tools to promote good governance.
- We illustrate how developing countries are integrating such considerations—as service accountability, open government, and access to government information for accountability—into their comprehensive e-government programs. How transparency should be phased into service delivery? How can accountability be embedded into government reform and modernization programs? How can ICT be leveraged to reinvent government, both from the top down and the bottom up?

Overview

ICT opens opportunities to broaden the reach of citizens' voices (citizen demands and legitimacy) and encourage and enable a response from the state to improve public services. It provides citizens a platform to demand services and a channel for feedback and evaluation of services. It can support government performance for service delivery and accountability through resource management transparency (for example, via budget tracking), process transparency (decision tracking), and performance accountability (performance indicators; user feedback).

ICT offers a platform for gathering and providing information, both for the government and citizens. It can foster a form of bottom-up transparency. In East Africa, for example, the project Twaweza ("we can make it happen") is engaging citizens (service users) in collecting information on water, health, and education, using their mobile phones. This circumvents not only the government's inability to provide access to information on projects and services, but also its unwillingness (Arnold 2011).

These benefits cannot be realized overnight or by acting on one technology alone. Realizing the potential benefits requires strategies to mobilize citizens and increase their take-up rates of e-services, invest in complementary managerial innovations and user connectivity, and incorporate complementary measures for strengthening DFGG. Bottom-up transparency also requires increasing the awareness and capacity of citizens and social intermediaries to engage and hold their governments accountable. ICT is not a solution to everything that is wrong with governance, accountability, and participation but it opens opportunities and new channels for transforming public services and innovating governance.

Digital government can be considered a form of government accountability designed to improve public services while at the same time providing increased information and transparency. E-government projects constitute major investments and a growing part of public service investment and development finance. Incorporating transparency and DFGG tools into these projects would only add a little cost to needed investments. The link between digitizing government processes/services (e-government) and using ICT for governance must be secured not only to leverage e-government investments for enhanced transparency and accountability, but also to secure sustained improvement in service delivery through continuous citizen and business feedback.

Public sector reforms to improve governance may be pursued by using ICT to: (i) reduce corruption by tracking budgets and revenues, making public procurement open and transparent, and mapping and monitoring critical resources; (ii) manage performance by using performance and service delivery indicators and tracking decisions and outcomes; (iii) engage citizens in policy development and facilitate citizen participation in development planning and implementation through effective decentralization; and (iv) enforce the rule of law and modernize the legislative and judicial branches of government.

Informing citizens of how public resources are spent is key to reducing waste and fraud. A growing number of states are using e-budgets in ways that allow viewers to choose general overviews of state spending in different policy areas, drill into detailed data sets, or compare actual results to desired results. This requires leadership to overcome resistance from those who fear that e-budgeting's democratizing effect could reduce their power and monopoly over knowledge about any inner workings or budgeted projects' actual performance. Nongovernmental organizations (NGOs) and civil society organizations (CSOs) can play a key role in pressing for access to such information, and in tracking and interpreting such information for a broader audience of stakeholders.

A key to reducing corruption is to make information on corruption-prone public services and processes readily available, for instance, by putting them online and making them monitorable and searchable.[1] For example, e-procurement can be a key tool to enable transparency and fight corruption, and at the same time, improve the efficiency and effectiveness of the public procurement function. But it is not a magic bullet or technical fix. Many vested interests are at stake. Corrupt practices in public procurement are supported by strong underlying networks involving private suppliers and public officials. Procurement reforms—to

---

[1] In countries or areas where Internet penetration is low, effective access to information may require social intermediaries that possess the effective hardware and skills to retrieve and interpret this information and then find ways that are not dependent on an Internet connection to disseminate this information.

promote efficiency, transparency, and accountability—may thus involve building countervailing coalitions that include reform-minded officials and civil servants from the executive branches of government, as well as leaders from the legislature, business, media, supreme audit institutions, and CSOs. Sharing relevant information via mobile phone is one way to strengthen demand for accountability and transparency in public procurement. Political leadership and social control are essential to success.

E-participation tools (including applications for mobile phones) can be used to engage citizens and businesses and seek their views so their interests and needs are better represented in government programs and processes. E-participation includes online surveys and polls, electronic newsletters, e-mail, feedback forms, and web forums where citizens can express their opinions. E-participation tools may supplement public forums or meetings. They may present relevant background information, decisions, and other materials to help citizens and businesses understand certain public policies or regulatory issues. The goal is to increase the responsiveness of the government to citizens and businesses.

It takes intense and sustained pressure from outside groups for governments to become open and let the sunshine in. Korea's Seoul municipal government subjected its key administrative procedures to public scrutiny through a searchable index of permit applications. Feedback or citizen comments and complaints also support anticorruption measures. For example, the Philippine Civil Service Commission (CSC) implemented a TXT CSC service that enables citizens to SMS or text in complaints regarding poor-quality services or corruption charges against government officials. The CSC must respond to queries within one day. Mobile-phone users can report grievances against the police using SMS. TXT CSC has also been used in a public service delivery audit in which citizens rated public services via text message.

Looking at the potential of using mobile solutions for good governance purposes, the possibilities are endless. Access to mobile phones empowers the individual in many ways as it opens up channels for a two-way dialogue between the government and the public. Mobile phones increase efficiency in daily activities as they help in time management and general organization. Mobile phones, together with social media such as Facebook, also hold a great potential for mobilization, coordination, and collective action among ordinary citizens. Mobile banking and mobile money-transfer systems such as M-Pesa (an application initiated in Kenya) and ZAP (found in many Sub-Saharan African countries) open up even greater opportunities and possibilities for transactions and bill/loan/fine payments for a variety of public services such as transport and school fees, as well as making it easier to hold the government accountable by making transactions more transparent.

Governance, Functions, Applications, Examples

As potential ICT applications for public services transformation and good governance are vast and varied, Table 3.1 organizes them by relevant governance and service function and lists relevant ICT uses. Selected examples are given from Africa, as the continent presents some of the greatest challenges in regard to governance, weak institutions, service deficit, and poor communication infrastructure. Most e-government applications span several objectives and services and serve both supply and demand measures to reform and strengthen governance and innovation in public services. These examples are only illustrative since ICT applications in each key government function and service are growing in diversity and increasingly spanning the fundamental objectives of public sector reforms.[2] In fact, there is a huge and growing number of applications indigenous to each continent and relevant to governance and public service delivery issues.

---

[2] *See* Hanna (2010). There are numerous examples of successful e-governance applications in both developed and developing countries and several compilations of case studies. Sources include the Affiliated Network for Social Accountability (ANSA-Africa) and various studies by Transparency International. InfoDev's e-government toolkit (www.egov.infodev.org) provides examples and resources covering e-government services and applications. The United Nations Department of Economic and Social Affairs (UNDESA), "Compendium of Innovative e-Government Practices," has been issued in two volumes: Vol. I (2005) and Vol. II (2006). Another is the e-government library and other resources of the United National Online Network in Public Administration and Finance (UNPAN). A third useful resource is the UN's annual Global e-Government Readiness Reports (published annually since 2004), which provide quantitative measures as well as illustrative examples of successful e-government projects. Finally, the e-Government Good Practice Framework compiles examples of portals, services, and resources from the developed countries of the European Union (EU). But almost all of these sources focus on the supply side to improve government services and governance, with little attention so far to the demand side.

Table 3.1 ICT Tools and Their Relevance to Specific Government Functions (with Examples from Africa)

Governance categories	Government functions/ application areas	Examples from Africa
1. Resource management and planning	• Budget and expenditure management • Integrated financial management systems (IFMSs) • E-taxes and e-customs • Human resources management • Disbursement of salaries and benefits • Natural resource management • Public procurement • Contracting out (public-private partnerships, outsourcing) • Monitoring of government contracts • E-procurement monitoring and analysis	**The Budget Tracking Tool (Kenya)** www.sodnet.org *A collaborative platform for grassroots communities to actively engage in public resource management.* **Celpay Conader Project (DRC)** www.celpay.com *This is a mobile money-transfer payment system for compensating demobilized soldiers.* **Map Kibera (Kenya)** www.mapkiberia.org *Kibera, known as Africa's largest slum in Nairobi, Kenya, remains a blank spot on the map. This monitoring and resource agent serves as an important accountability tool.* **LiberFor (Liberia)** www.liberfor.com *System to manage forest resources in a structured and sustainable manner to prevent illegal logging.* **mWater (Senegal)** www.pepam.gouv.sn/ www.manobi.net *This basic monitoring service via mobile phones helps in data transmission, analysis, and dialogue between rural water scheme operators and regulatory agents, thus ensuring continuation of water delivery, management of water resources, and follow-up for supporting operations.*

| 2. Services to citizens | • Government information services
• Government call centers, kiosks
• Citizen scorecards
• Social networking, SMS feedback
• Citizen-centered, one-stop services
• Health services
• Education services
• Water and sanitation services
• Social security benefits
• Permits and licenses
• Registrations
• Birth and marriage certificates
• Payment of salaries and benefits
• Employment/job search
• Building permits
• Participation in local governance
• Analytics applied to call centers
• Demand for services and citizen feedback | **Raising the Water Pressure, Maji Matone (Tanzania)**
www.daraja.org
This nongovernmental organization (NGO) aims to develop tools and encourage citizens to report water functionalities in their areas.

Stop Stockouts (Kenya, Malawi, Uganda, Zambia, Zimbabwe)
www.stopstockouts.org
Using the Ushahidi crowdsourcing platform and FrontlineSMS, researchers during "pill check week" send data to a common site to indicate areas in the map where medication is out of stock.

Jokko Initiative (Senegal)
www.jokkoinitiative.org
Jokko means "communication" or "dialogue" in local dialect Wolof; in partnership with the United Nations Children's Fund (UNICEF) it focuses on empowering rural communities to use mobile technology.

Media Focus on Africa
www.mediafocusonafrica.org
This organization was founded on the premise that the free flow of information will build better societies on issues such as development and democratization.

Kubatana Trust (Zimbabwe)
www.kubatana.net/
An exhaustive database of articles and reports on civic information and human rights, plus a directory of civil society organizations (CSOs) and social justice groups.

CU@School (Uganda)
twaweza.org
The organization Twaweza, in collaboration with SNV Uganda, addresses teacher absenteeism and pupil attendance using an SMS messaging system. The pilot will be used in 100 primary schools in 2 districts informing government officials to take action. |

Continued

Table 3.1 ICT Tools and Their Relevance to Specific Government Functions (with Examples from Africa) (Continued)

Governance categories	Government functions/ application areas	Examples from Africa
3. Services to business	• E-licenses and e-permits • E-reporting (statistics) • Extension services for farmers • Extension services to small and medium enterprises (SMEs) • E-transactions through mobile phones, portals • Monitoring enforcement of regulation • Public procurement • Corporate tax payment • Customs declaration • Trade facilitation • E-customs and e-patents • Land records • Business analytics and data mining applied to government transactions with business	**Ghana Customs Portal** www.gcnet.com.gh/ *A portal set up by the Government of Ghana to facilitate and answer all queries related to customs and trade.* **M-Pesa (Kenya)** www.safaricom.co.ke/index.php?id=250 *This mobile money-payment-transfer system is the biggest success story in mobile applications in Sub-Saharan Africa for improving access to financial and other services to microbusinesses and citizens.*

| 4. Political accountability | • Parliamentary and judicial system websites
• Local governance participation through crowdsourcing, other portals
• Elections monitoring
• SMS reports, social networking for accountability
• e-Cabinet
• Election monitoring
• Data mining tools
• Grievance mechanisms, ombudsman
• Audit institutions
• e-municipalities | **Mzalendo (Kenya)**
www.mzalendo.com
This volunteer-run project, meaning "patriot" in Kiswahili, began in 2005 with the mission to "keep an eye on the Kenyan Parliament."
Ushahidi (Kenya)
www.ushahidi.com
Ushahidi maps incidents through crowdsourcing data to generate quick information that complements data from official monitors of elections.
Liberia Corruption Watch (Liberia)
http://www.cental.org/
An initiative of the Centre for Transparency and Accountability in Liberia (CENTAL), this website acts as a repository of corruption stories reported by the media.
Kleptocracy Fighters, Inc. (Uganda)
www.kfighters.com
KFighters allows citizens to record and report real-time information on government corruption through audio, video, and text messages.
African Elections Project
www.africanelections.org
An online portal monitoring elections in 10 African countries in 3 languages (English, French, and Portuguese).
It was used in the 2011 referendum.
The Ujima Project
http://ujima-project.org/
This is an online repository of data sets, including information on weapons sales and funds from foreign governments and organizations, accessible to citizens and journalists in Africa. |

Resource Management

Managing public resources (financial, human, natural, informational) is a core function of the government and is at the forefront of the development and competitiveness agendas of many countries. Pressed by increasing budgetary constraints, rising expectations and demand for services and accountability, and meeting the imperatives of a global economy, governments are seeking to become agile, promote managerial flexibility, and harness their financial and human resources. At the same time, taxpayers and businesses have a major stake in ensuring accountability, transparency, efficiency, and effectiveness in managing scarce public resources—to reduce tax burdens, and the cost of doing business with the government. This is an area where ICT has made substantial contributions in the finance and private sectors, and the potential is vast and relatively untapped for the public sector.

Reform objectives of improving public sector efficiency and resource management can be enabled by ICT uses and applications that: (i) improve public resource mobilization and expenditure management through tax modernization, integrated financial management systems (IFMSs), and budget tracking and expenditure monitoring; (ii) improve human resource management information and processes, and facilitate civil service reforms and performance management; (iii) increase competitiveness, reduce transaction costs, and increase transparency of public procurement with electronic procurement applications; (iv) focus and downsize government through increased employee productivity and transparent contracting, outsourcing, and partnerships with the private sector and civil society; and (v) improve program management and reengineer government processes to make them more responsive and transparent; enable oversight; and reduce fraud, and bypass corrupt intermediaries, or make them obsolete.

The most common of ICT applications in support of resource management are those concerning *financial resource mobilization and expenditure management*, including treasury systems, tax and customs administration, and Integrated Financial Management Systems (IFMSs). Integrated treasury systems, for example, offer significant benefits in managing public resources, including real-time information on the funds available to the state, greater financial control, improved financial transparency and accountability, better reporting at various levels of budget execution, sound planning for future requirements, and better data for budget formulation. IFMSs can become the backbone for broad managerial improvement and government transformation. Pressures from the global financial system, aid agencies, and ministries of finance often make IFMS applications an attractive entry point for ICT-enabled policy and institutional reform.[3]

A recent review of programs to strengthen public financial management in postconflict countries acknowledged that attention to citizen engagement and domestic accountability mechanisms tends to be considered too late, if at all (PREM 2011). The same review suggests that stronger reform emphasis on transparency measures, accountability institutions, and the engagement of civil society could enhance state legitimacy and help sustain the demand for public financial management reforms. Such approaches may also have political appeal if they help government secure greater public credit for reform efforts.

Online budget tracking and mobile tools can be harnessed to improve community engagement in local development planning and public resource management. If the government is not transparent enough, social intermediaries and community organizations can step in and begin to publish government data themselves. They can do this by attending parliamentary sessions, reporting and making the content public, or by browsing and scanning government websites for information and presenting them in an understandable, visual way. Social intermediaries can further help augment demand for budget accountability, by analyzing budget allocations in terms of target groups and locations, using analytics and geomapping tools, and by visualizing and presenting information such that they are accessible to communities and beneficiaries.

A budget tracking tool (Kenya, http://transparency.globalvoicesonline.org/project/budget-tracking-tool) draws information from the Kenyan

---

[3] Including meeting standards prescribed under various international standards and codes, such as the International Monetary Fund (IMF) code of Good Practice on Fiscal Transparency, Declaration on Principles, and the fiduciary standards of the World Bank. Of course, these systems are only enablers and not a substitute for the necessary and accompanying policies and institutional reforms.

Community Development Fund and provides online budgetary data for all constituency-level development projects in Kenya. This tool receives most of its budgetary data from the government and in part relies on data provided by partner NGOs. It automatically responds to information requests and sends detailed budgetary information for specific projects via e-mail or short message service (SMS). Then it aggregates the information and presents it online in a searchable and user-friendly manner. This tool is primarily oriented toward established NGOs and civil groups that are active in the constituencies and capable of confronting local politicians in cases of potential corruption.

The tool enables citizens to search for project funds, information on schools and hospitals, and types of funds and allocation summaries, and to do benefit mapping. It also enables citizens to anonymously report problems about project implementation and incidences of corruption. It enables civil society members to network and leaders to dialogue with citizens and lobby groups.

An example of ICT application to strengthen the demand for good governance is *mapping and monitoring the needs and resources of poor communities.* Kibera in Nairobi, Kenya—widely known as Africa's largest slum—remains a blank spot on the map. Without basic knowledge of the geography and resources of Kibera, it is impossible to have an informed discussion on how to improve the lives of residents. In November 2009, young Kiberans created the first public digital map of their own community. Map Kibera runs a Wiki (presenting community plans), discussion forums (using Google Group, Facebook, Twitter), and community media (called Voice of Kibera). They also run the Community Tracking and Mapping of Constituency Development Fund project, which allows Kenyans to easily view both official and on-the-ground details of the Constituency Development Fund (CDF) projects that are ongoing in Kibera. The application reviews and maps submitted reports on the real status of aid and development projects on the ground, in contrast to official government reports, as well as allocated amounts, contractor details, photographs, and geographic locations. This evidence-based monitoring, combined with the communication power of maps and the web, serves as a powerful advocacy tool for improved accountability of development funds in Kenya.

Another example of mapping and monitoring the needs and resources of poor communities comes from a mobile-phone survey in South Sudan. It demonstrates in dramatic ways how mobile phones can be used even under very difficult conditions and with limited infrastructure to assess conditions concerning material deprivation and personal security at the cusp of independence. The objectives of this application are to assess poverty conditions, monitor the situation, and draw lessons on the use of mobile-phone surveys.

Another area of increasing attraction that could potentially promise vast gains for transparency and efficiency is *e-government procurement* (e-GP). This is a proven application that has been successfully implemented in several developing countries, with a wide range of benefits. It is a key area of transparency reform with low financial costs and high benefits. Experience so far suggests that electronic procurement can save as much as 20 percent of the costs of publicly procured goods and services, by increasing competition, reducing prices, reducing corruption, lowering transaction process costs, and practicing smart procurement (using analytics tools). Electronic public procurement can widen fair competition, increase transparency and accountability, lower inventory costs, speed transactions, and support policy analysis and public financial management (Box 3.1).

Chile's e-procurement system (Chilecompra or "Chile buys") is often cited as a success. It is credited with making government procurement more transparent, reducing businesses' transaction costs, enhancing cooperation between firms and public agencies, and reducing opportunities for corruption. Chile used e-procurement as a key entry point to fighting corruption. It used data mining of e-procurement transactions, among other tools, to avoid bid rigging, and to break up collusive practices among suppliers, officials, and procurement officers.

Under Chile's e-procurement system, companies that wish to do business with the public sector only need to register once about areas in which they do business. Whenever a public agency needs to purchase goods or services, it will fill out a request in the electronic system, specifying the kind of operation and including all the documentation and information associated with the request. The system automatically sends an e-mail to all the private companies registered in that area, minimizing response

Box 3.1

E-Procurement, Transparency, Accountability, and Participation

According to the 2009 Global Corruption Report published by Transparency International, corruption in public procurement raised project costs by approximately 10 percent, resulting in a loss of $300–500 billion around the world.

In the past 15 years, public procurement reform, enabled by ICT and process simplification, has created a wealth of knowledge and products in the e-GP domain. Information disclosure through public access to procurement data is improving government accountability and control of public expenditure. All stages of the procurement process can benefit from electronic processes, including prequalification, advertising, preparation and issuance of bidding documents, receipt of bids, bid opening, evaluation of bids, clarification and modification, and notification and publication of results. In most developing countries, these steps are carried out manually, often resulting in delays in the process and increases in associated costs and corruption. Many countries have embarked on e-procurement programs: from Korea, Singapore, Australia, Canada, and the United States to Chile, Brazil, India, and the Philippines.

The benefits of e-procurement include increased transparency, efficiency, performance, and monitoring of public procurement. It improves the accessibility of information and facilitates fiduciary compliance by automating practices prone to corruption. While many client countries have started to invest in e-procurement initiatives, the design and implementation of such programs can benefit from adopting best practices. Often, technological parameters are emphasized, while critical success factors are neglected. But improvements from applying e-procurement are not an automatic or one-time event. Rather, e-procurement involves a learning process that requires change management, stakeholder engagement, coalition building, identification of "quick wins," phasing and sequencing, and other measures to secure government and citizen-led accountability measures and realize the potential benefits of investing in the technology.

Source: Author.

time and providing an equal opportunity for all firms. At the end of the bidding process, the results are provided online, including details on the participants, the proposals, the economic and technical scores, and the winning contractor. This improves transparency, accountability, and participation in public procurement.

Although the benefits of e-procurement can be clearly measurable and even dramatic, and thus attractive to private investment or public–private partnerships (PPPs), these benefits are not automatic (Box 3.2). Realizing the payoffs depends on complementary infrastructure, supplier incentives, user capacity, coalition building, change management, and demand-driven measures for transparency, among others. In the Philippines, a coalition of CSOs was essential to enact a new procurement law embodying key reforms, and to continue to provide oversight over implementation, using e-procurement to make the process transparent and amenable to monitoring.

Governance can be enhanced by *modernizing tax systems and revenue administration*. Tax administration, tax policy analysis, and taxpayer services are being transformed under e-government programs as well. The challenges and benefits of the use of ICT in tax modernization do not start or end with tax reporting and payment. In fact, many of the benefits come from the quantum leaps in administrative reforms and productivity increases that result from transforming back-end processes to improve government productivity in administering and processing taxes as well as improvements in services and reductions in transaction costs to businesses and citizens. ICT also has the potential to improve tax policy analysis, compliance, and the detection of tax fraud.

Box 3.2

E-Government Procurement: Demand and Supply Measures to Improve Service and Governance

E-government procurement can improve procurement services and at the same time provide technological and institutional platforms to improve transparency and accountability for public procurement. One interesting example of mobilizing demand for the reform of public procurement comes from the Philippines. The legal foundation for procurement was fragmented, with over 100 laws and regulations. A new omnibus law was needed to bring clarity and predictability to the process, and to provide an enabling environment for investing in e-procurement systems. The law, enacted in 2003, was the result of determined efforts of officials allied with unified advocacy efforts of civil society organizations (CSOs), designed to offset entrenched vested interests. Passing laws and investing in systems, however, are not enough to secure the intended results. Credible enforcement and oversight institutions are essential. In this case, all bids and awards committees must have at least an observer from a certified CSO. To enable CSOs to fulfill their role, CSO observers receive extensive training.

The e-procurement application may illustrate the critical success factors for e-government applications in general. These factors include both demand and supply measures, with the most determining factors on the demand side. On the demand side, strong political leadership and commitment, and sustainable coalition for reforming public procurement and fighting corruption are essential. This support must materialize in terms of appropriate procurement laws and regulations, and social, political, and judicial oversight to make sure the laws are applied, and transparency enforced by e-procurement. The ministry of finance, parliament, and CSOs can be crucial allies to secure value for public money.

On the supply side, e-procurement should be developed in line with local capacity for institutional and technological change—fitting into the technological and connectivity infrastructure of government, phasing implementation in line with political commitment and the e-readiness of various government agencies, and accompanied with process reengineering, providing incentives, managing change, training and communicating with the midlevel managers involved in procurement, outsourcing, or partnering with the private sector as may be appropriate, mandating the publication of tenders, and developing mechanisms for the enforcement of regulations and resolution of conflicts.

Source: Author.

One final critical area of public resource management is *human resource management,* a relatively underdeveloped area of public service management and governance. This function is essential to realize substantial gains in productivity, upgrade civil service skills and services, align incentives to performance, increase accountability, and enable overall change and transformation of government. The integration of human resource management functions such as competency-based training and promotion system are enabled by interlinked ICT applications: the HRM System, Learning Management System (LMS), Learning Content Management System (LCMS), e-training, and so on. Given the poor state of information about the civil services of many developing countries, these applications could offer the powerful tools needed for governments to manage a modern civil service and hold it accountable.

Services to Citizens

Improving the access and quality of public services is a political, social, and economic imperative for all developing countries. This is understandable in view of rising expectations for better public services, large deficits in access and quality of such services, and the high transaction costs of dealing with unwieldy bureaucracies. Governments often face the difficult trade-off between improving service quality to those who are better off, mainly in urban areas, and extending access to those with limited or no access, particularly the poor and those living in rural areas. E-government applications can deliver on both quality and access, while enhancing transparency, accountability, and participation.

Policy makers and public sector leaders can use ICT-enabled improvements in key services to build trust, strengthen demand for good governance, and provide external support for broader government reforms. This support could come from business associations, private groups, organized citizenry, or, more broadly, the electorate. Unlike using e-government for transparency, participatory democracy, and other visions, an initial focus on service improvement is the least threatening to the social and political status quo. An initial emphasis on service delivery can be a neutral entry point to building longer-term political support for performance improvement and government transformation (West 2005).

ICT-enabled service delivery is a rich category with many examples of innovative applications to:

- Improve the availability, quality, and responsiveness of public services such as the supply of water, land titles, licenses, permits, and certificates.
- Support health, education, and lifelong learning.
- Provide choice and competition in service delivery through information brokerage and the use of PPPs.
- Reduce transaction costs to citizens by providing one-stop service centers, user-friendly mobile applications, single windows, and citizen-centric portals, among others.

A key route to improving the availability and quality and responsiveness of public services is to augment citizen monitoring and feedback. *Huduma*, for example, is an interactive, multimedia tool that channels and amplifies citizens' concerns, complaints, and suggestions directly to service providers, policy makers, and budget holders (Box 3.3). Another example illustrates the key point that citizens' monitoring of service delivery can deploy a combination of communication tools for maximum results (Box 3.3). In Uganda a multimedia platform combines popular media such as radio talk shows with data visualization and geocoding,

Box 3.3

Citizen Reporting via Huduma (Kenya) and via TRAC FM (Uganda)

Huduma is a Swahili word for "service," developed by SODNET, which is an indigenous organization established by NGO workers in Kenya. Huduma is an interactive, multimedia tool that channels and amplifies citizens' concerns, complaints, and suggestions directly to service providers, policy makers, and budget holders. The platform is available online to the public through www.huduma.info and incorporates easy visualization and interactive tools for media and citizen engagement. In each county, the action will work with civil society and professional groups as a means of verifying "crowd" or "citizen" demands. The media will have a critical role in highlighting instances of lapses, concerns, and best possible practices. The channels (SMS, Web, radio, TV, churches, mosques) allow citizens to report (for example, lack of medicines, potholes, lack of teachers, broken water points and so on) to a Huduma channel, mostly an SMS number.

The voice or concern is then amplified to the respective authority via Web, e-mail, and SMS while simultaneously being visualized on a Web platform. The overall thematic areas for reporting are health, education, and water. Governance and infrastructure also feature as themes in Huduma as they are intrinsic to service delivery. Reporting and feedback are mainly managed through the Huduma channels to ensure a historic thread of the conversation until the problem is resolved or deferred.

In collaboration with a media house, TRAC FM identifies common service delivery problems in Uganda. Based on the problem and in line with software requirements, survey questions are formulated, such as, "Which street in Kampala has the worst potholes?" During a radio show broadcast, the presenter asks the question of his listeners and asks them to send in a free SMS to 8585 containing the name of the street. Listeners could reply with keyword "repair" followed by the street name "Ntinda Rd." The answer would thus be "repair Ntinda road." Next, the message "repair Ntinda road" is collected in a database and processed into a data visualization. The radio presenter can see what listeners are messaging while presenting the show. So he can inform people that Ntinda road has eight reports with roads with the worst potholes.

Data collected during the radio surveys will be used, along with relevant background information, in an "info graphic" that is published in the Daily Monitor every month. A map of Kampala with the worst potholes is highlighted, along with additional text written by an editor of the publication. The information will also be available online through various Web sites and TRAC FM's Facebook page.

The reach of radio networks and the uptake of mobile technology by Ugandan citizens allows for unprecedented involvement, openness, and vibrancy in public debate. TRAC FM builds on the success of interactive radio platforms and aims to stimulate an informed political debate outside the domain of the political elite.

Source: www.sodnet.org/index.php?option=com_content&view=article&id=139: huduma-a-step-ahead-in-the-journey-of-reforms (for Huduma).

which allows for a new and efficient form of citizen monitoring. It identifies common problems (such as teacher absenteeism, drug stockouts, potholes, and so on) and the public interacts via radio and mobiles to analyze and debate service delivery problems and solutions.

One scarce resource and critical service is *water supply* to rural areas. The Tanzanian NGO Daraja aims to develop tools and encourage citizens to report water point functionality in their areas. An SMS-based feedback mechanism has been developed for citizens to report on the state of rural water supply. The information provided is forwarded to the relevant government authorities—thus enabling them to respond quickly—as well as to the media. It is promoted through radio and newspapers. Twaweza, a local NGO, is providing support to Daraja to (i) share information about water point functionality with the public in accessible formats, primarily through the media; (ii) enable citizens to update functionality information in real time via SMS; and (iii) analyze and publicize responsiveness of government to citizen notification.

Public delivery of *education services* can be made transparent and accountable by empowering stakeholders with information and monitoring tools. For example, research indicates that primary school teachers in a number of African countries are absent from school 15–25 percent of the time, and that many of those in school are not found teaching. Twaweza, in collaboration with SNV Uganda, is trying to address this problem. The project facilitates monitoring of teacher and pupil attendance and absenteeism in primary schools by using an SMS-based information system. The project pilots an SMS application that generates frequent and detailed overviews of teacher and pupil attendance in 100 primary schools in two districts. The information will make the dynamics around teacher absenteeism transparent and will inform district and subdistrict government officials on appropriate short-, medium-, and long-term action, as well as nonstate actors at (sub)district levels.

Yet, technology is not a panacea for educational reforms, as social institutions determine the usefulness of technology. A case study of introducing educational satellite television in Ethiopia shows that information and participation are critical to the introduction of new technologies in service delivery, and the absence of such information leads to mass alienation and apathy (Box 3.4). The case shows that the government

Box 3.4

Access to Information and Service Delivery: Educational Satellite Television in Ethiopia

In 2005, the Ethiopian government started adopting ICT to maximize the delivery of education services. Government officials expected ICT to solve the lack of qualified teachers and the poor quality of education in secondary schools. The program that incorporated ICT delivery is called School Net. Its objective is to transform education by connecting all public high schools in the country to its network. Satellite television instruction is one component of School Net. The government allocated $70.6 million to satellite TV instruction, indicating the priority given to implementing this technology in schools.

The program involved two primary activities: (i) building the infrastructure and producing educational materials, and (ii) building human capacity. The first activity included the production of about 3,000 TV programs filmed in South Africa, the supply of electricity to schools, and the installation of satellite-receiving devices—plasma display panels and satellite dish receivers (V-Sats) in every school. The second activity entailed broadcasting prerecorded lessons according to a fixed schedule from the Educational Mass-Media Agency. Each class program mimicked an actual lesson with the on-screen instructor, who taught basic concepts and referred students to exercises in accompanying guidebooks.

But the outcome has been the opposite: the deterioration of students' educational experience. The primary reasons are: (i) the government made this change without transparency or consultation with any stakeholders, even teachers and students; and (ii) technology has serious limitations such as the fast speed and unfamiliar language of the instructors, power interruption, malfunctioning TV sets, and lack of relevant content. The lack of interactivity has made technology a weak substitute for traditional face-to-face teaching. It has undermined student-centered education by denying students the opportunity to participate and engage in the learning process. Teachers were also unhappy with their roles being limited to switching the TV on and off.

The case shows that the government needs to improve the flow of information throughout the school system. It must provide mechanisms for students, teachers, and parents to provide feedback, make suggestions, and report complaints that will be acted upon by the government. Students' councils and teachers' associations could be given the latitude to act on their members' views. Schools must also take steps to ensure parent participation. Information gaps between users and officials can be bridged, and demand-driven service delivery will occur when the government nurtures and promotes CSOs and encourages the media to report on all issues.

The government plans to broadcast the educational program via an Internet-streamed digital video. This method will give more control to teachers—to prescreen, slow down, or fast forward each broadcast. But the fundamental problems will remain. The main interest of the students is to have more face-to-face interaction with their teachers, while teachers want more time to exercise their profession: teaching or sharing their knowledge with their students. Lacking this opportunity, the Internet system may remain technology driven with little human interaction in the teaching-learning process.

Source: Tegegne Gebre Egziabher in Kpundeh, Khadiagala, and Chowdhury (2008).

needs to improve the flow of information throughout the school system. It shows that mechanisms must be deployed for students, teachers, and parents to provide feedback, make suggestions, and report complaints that will be acted upon by the government.

Health service delivery also suffers from weak information on the supply and demand sides. Take the case of the supply of drugs to public health facilities in Kenya. It shows how weak information on the supply side constrains planning, and procurement engenders wastage and drug stock outages. At the warehousing and distribution stage, inadequate information on the supply and distribution of drugs, compounded by poor stock management systems in the health facilities, creates loopholes for pilferage, especially where institutional governance is weak. On the demand side, perpetual drug outages have eroded citizens' confidence in public health facilities. The lack of information about the reforms to improve drug supply, and actual availability of essential drugs at health facilities has resulted in low use of public health facilities. Without adequate information, citizens cannot demand their rights to health care. The information vacuum deepens public mistrust of the public health system.

E-government portals and open data can help citizens make informed decisions by sharing and widely distributing the information they collect about the public and private sector. One of the most vital roles for government in the information society is to act as an information broker. The Internet, and information kiosks in the case of developing countries, can facilitate this role by aggregating and distributing information about access, quality, and price of any service—public or private. For example, some state governments in the United States have compiled online report cards on schools to enable parents to make informed choices about their children's educational options, and at the same time, to expose schools to public pressure for improved performance (Eggers 2005).

Other ways to facilitate markets and improve service choice for citizens is to deploy eBay-like feedback mechanisms to allow consumers of public services to rate various services and providers. Similar public report cards have been introduced online for hospitals, and surveys have been developed by NGOs for a few Indian cities to rate the services of local public agencies. These surveys had a perceptible impact on performance and accountability in these localities, and can now be extended and shared online and at kiosks.

Around the world, government portals are providing points of entry for reshaping, reorganizing, and recreating governments—virtually. Appropriately organized around citizens needs, and increasingly made amenable to citizen-driven personalization, these portals usher in the era of seamless government, or "government without walls." Accordingly, citizens and business can transact with multiple agencies and multiple levels of government in a single place or portal. The web presence of the government is organized around terms familiar to citizens', such as life events or target groups, thus eliminating the need for citizens to decipher the increasingly complex and incomprehensible organizations of government or to pay bribes for access.

More broadly and for all types of services to citizens in developing countries, information on quality and cost is not available or difficult to obtain. The poor suffer the most from a lack of information, both as producers and consumers. Making information available through mobile phones, the Internet, and kiosks or infomediaries could help citizens weigh choices and allow better matching and flexibility to meet diverse needs and preferences. In some service areas and for some special populations, navigators or special guidance systems may be needed, and electronic matching systems may provide guidance to match needs. Publishing public data, transactions, and services on the web could enable other government agencies, the private sector, NGOs, and other infomediaries to integrate, package, or customize the information and services into their own service offerings, thereby providing additional choices and pathways into services. Several countries have initiated open government initiatives to make public information resources available to citizens and NGOs. This is potentially a powerful tool for enhancing transparency and accountability.

In developing countries, a wide range of basic services to citizens is in strong demand. Examples include: land and property registration, birth registration, driver licensing, automobile registration, employment, education, professional training, pensions, health services, tax reporting and payment, and visa services. Popular services include school and exam results, health services appointments, and information on women's health. In many developing countries, and particularly in Latin America, public safety is a major issue, and in response, some of the emerging uses of ICT include online crime reporting, police electronic records, and crime mapping. Many such services can be delivered through mobile phones, kiosks, or community information centers.

Many of these services may require significant improvements in back-end processes to provide reliable service and completed transactions, particularly in the context of many developing countries where the first wave of computerization and process reengineering has not been advanced. The challenge in developing countries is not only to put services online or make information available on mobile phones, but also to carry out the internal process transformation and integration necessary to enable complete transactions of such services. This calls for prioritization and sequencing of e-services to ensure that the transformation process is not aborted by limiting e-government to web presence or window dressing.

But applying ICT to improve processes for service delivery does not go far enough in improving service delivery unless it is also used to build demand for improved transparency and accountability, and thus overcome mistrust in government decision making and service delivery. The case of financing higher education in Kenya shows that efficient service delivery depends on how well institutions manage and share information with beneficiaries (Box 3.5).

Many countries are transferring more responsibilities and resources to the *local government* levels as most service delivery to citizens occurs here. Effective delivery of such services via mobile and community information centers can accelerate improvements and build trust in the government.

Box 3.5

Transparency and Service Quality in Financing Higher Education in Kenya

Education is a key pillar of economic development and poverty reduction in Kenya and accounts for about 35 percent of total government spending and 7 percent of GDP. In addition to the direct financing of university programs, the government provides loans and bursaries to needy students. An autonomous agency, the Higher Education Loans Board (HELB), administers this program. The organization's model of information sharing and service delivery is being replicated in neighboring countries such as Lesotho, Rwanda, Tanzania, Uganda, and Zimbabwe.

To reach potential new beneficiaries, the HELB calls for applications through media advertisements and intermediary institutions, addresses the assembly of head teachers who are in contact with the students before they leave school, publishes a magazine, and maintains a Web site with information on the board's mandate and loan application process. Every year the board processes close to 40,000 applications. A loan qualification committee has developed a mean-testing formula and points system for awarding finance. The HELB disburses loans with two main components: tuition fees and students' maintenance. It operates loan processing, disbursement, appeal, and recovery. A student can access information about their disbursement through the Web site www.helb.co.ke, via SMS, by e-mailing the HELB office, by telephone inquiry, or through the dean's offices of respective universities.

In its 2002–2007 strategic plan, the HELB identified enhanced information systems as key to its operations. The board invested heavily in ICT, computerizing its operations and launching a new interactive Web site. Current and past borrowers seeking information on their loan status could access the online database, reducing the number of physical visits to the office as well as the board's paperwork. Other services available on the Web included: regular transmission of data to the universities, inquiries on loan repayment and production of statements for all borrowers, loan payments through e-commerce facilities, and various queries answered online.

Information gaps between the HELB and beneficiaries remain: (i) the board requires students to provide truthful information about family income (similarly, students also doubt the objectivity of the selection process), (ii) the HELB could improve information about the application process via various media though the investment in ICT had improved the dissemination process, and (iii) the appeals process is slow and can extend into the following semester before a verdict is reached.

The case shows that efficient service delivery depends on how well institutions manage and share information with beneficiaries. Mistrust among the stakeholders reinforces the case for more transparency and information sharing. Investments in ICT-facilitated operations have not been leveraged enough for trust and transparency: for example, sharing a means-testing and postqualification formula for appeals and disclosing it on the application form and on the Web site; displaying the loan amount awarded to each student on university notice boards and/or on the Web; demystifying the eligibility criteria, and so on.

Source: By Jane Kiringai and James Njeru, in Kpundeh, Khadiagala, and Chowdhury (2008).

E-government may be used to support such decentralization processes by increasing the efficiency and transparency of local governments, as well as by improving information and service delivery. Specific measures may include mobile-phone apps, municipal portals, e-municipal procurement systems, cadaster and registration systems, and online forums.

Local and municipal governments are also offering localized and specialized government services. One survey of rural users of e-government in Madhya Pradesh, India, found the following services most in demand: personal documents, including birth, marriage, and death certificates; land registry or cadastral services; anticorruption complaints and other grievances with public services; and transportation related services, including car registration and purchase of bus and rail passes.

There is a growing body of evidence that demonstrates that *mobile money transfers* are effective in "ameliorating vulnerability and chronic poverty" and could also have wider positive impacts within recipient households and communities (Freeland and Vincent 2009). Some African governments have begun to leverage the mobile platform for paying salaries and for citizens to pay bills for various services such as water or electricity, and to transfer money directly to intended beneficiaries. For example, a Bank-funded project used mobile technology to provide direct payments for compensating demobilized soldiers in the Democratic Republic of Congo. The local authorities faced a challenge of preparing logistics to distribute monthly cash payments to over 100,000 ex-combatants. The banking system in the country was inadequate and nonexistent, yet the use of mobile technology was quickly growing. The company responsible for this application, Celpay, has operations in Zambia, the Democratic Republic of Congo, and is soon to launch operations in Tanzania (see www.celpay.com/).

Services to Business

The globally competitive economy is driving governments to improve their business climate and provide effective support services to their small and medium enterprises (SMEs). Public sector reforms aim to enhance transparency, reduce transaction costs to business, support entrepreneurship and SME development, and facilitate trade. These reform objectives are significantly enabled by e-government and mobile applications. This is a crucial area for Africa's future with its potential for employment generation, competitiveness, and broad-based growth. It is also critical to strengthening government capacity and accountability for effective and transparent resource management, and for engaging communities in resource-rich areas to ensure that environmental safeguards and benefits are responsive to their needs.

E-government offers many ways to improve the investment climate, business competitiveness, and business accountability and regulation. Electronic *public procurement*, for example, is an area where results can be demonstrated early and clearly in terms of efficiency, agility, and transparency. Beyond improving efficiency of government procurement operations, e-procurement can be designed to promote competition among a larger pool of suppliers and broaden the participation of SMEs in public procurement, and increase transparency and accountability. Whenever a public agency needs to purchase goods or contract a service, the system can automatically send an e-mail to all the private companies registered in that selected area, thus minimizing response time and providing an equal opportunity for all the firms. Results from procurement decisions can be shared over websites and mobiles.

In Karnataka, India, the Bhoomi land registry system has automated 20 million *land records* since its inception in 1998, yielding benefits to farmers, financial institutions, and public officials. Farmers, for example, can quickly get their land records from kiosks and are protected from harassment and extortion. Whereas getting records formerly entailed a delay of up to 30 days, farmers now get their records in less than 2 minutes. In this, as in other e-government applications, benefits include not only increased efficiency but also reduction in opportunities for corruption: making government services available to small farmers and small businesses in a transparent and efficient manner can also empower them against corrupt and arbitrary bureaucratic action.

Customs administration is another area of critical but costly transactions between government and businesses, and a major source for corruption, uncertainties and delays in clearance, and erosion in international competitiveness. It is a traditional area where the Bank has been active, with significant impact on governance and reducing corruption. But a lot needs to be done to mobilize DFGG and incorporate incentives and accountability measures for customs officers and administrations.

Many customs administrations have suffered from corruption and struggled to identify options for ameliorating this malady. In seeking to reduce corruption, while simultaneously strengthening performance (such as raising revenue collection and enhancing trade facilitation), policy makers should conduct experiments that can assist in identifying constructive policies.

One broad area of application is to use ICT to streamline *administrative procedures* so as to reduce transaction costs between businesses and government, and make these transactions transparent at the same time. Businesses and investors in developing countries are often frustrated by an inefficient and bureaucratic public sector; by high barriers to entry because of cumbersome, costly, and lengthy start-up processes; and by corruption and red tape. High transaction costs are particularly detrimental to small businesses and small investors with limited resources to pay such costs or to avoid them. Common government ICT applications to improve the business environment include e-registration, e-reporting, e-tax, and e-procurement.

An interactive online business registration system greatly simplifies the application processing and increases the speed of business registration, which currently can take more than 100 days in many developing countries. Even in the absence of e-signature infrastructure and an electronic payment system, investors may be given the possibility of downloading the necessary forms. The key is to provide a single platform allowing businesses to retrieve information and/or register with all the relevant public agencies, such as the state statistical office, agency for payments, tax authorities, customs authorities, and so on.

Municipal services play a key role in shaping the investment environment and the cost of doing business. Lessons should be drawn from using ICT to accelerate and sustain such reforms at the local level. Municipalities, as much as central governments, are competing to reduce their regulatory burdens and improve their transparency and attractiveness to businesses and investors (Box 3.6).

The second broad area of service delivery to businesses is to *promote investment and provide business support services.* Investment promotion may

Box 3.6

Municipal Scorecard on Business Climate, and the Role of ICT

The International Finance Corporation (IFC), in collaboration with local institutional partners including public, private, and academic institutions, conducted a pilot to produce the Municipal Scorecard 2007 (www.municipalscorecard.org). The pilot focused on two key processes—operating licenses and construction permits—in 65 municipalities in 5 Latin American countries. Most municipalities use the operating license to enforce zoning, health, and safety regulations; to acquire information about economic activities in their jurisdictions; and to improve tax control. Similarly, municipalities use construction permits to ensure that safety requirements are met and that building plans fit with urban development plans and building norms.

Unfortunately, businesses in many municipalities in developing countries report that licensing procedures are slow, expensive, and highly uncertain. Often, business owners cannot find the information they need to complete the process. They wait in long lines and are often asked to come back some other day. They are asked to pay very high fees to obtain a license, and worse, in some municipalities, they are asked for extra payments to speed up the process. To ensure their request is processed, most business owners have to leave their businesses and travel several times to municipal offices. High percentages of these licenses and permits are also rejected, in major part due to poor process management, starting with the poor quality of information that business owners receive, and the way in which requests must be presented.

To avoid these burdens, uncertainties and costs, many—particularly micro and small owners—prefer to remain unlicensed, that is, informal. Unfortunately, this means that society is left without adequate protection concerning zoning, health, and safety, and municipalities miss out on much-needed tax revenues. These informal businesses have fewer opportunities to grow, receive credit, take advantage of technology, increase productivity, and resist the grip of corruption.

Municipal transactions with business owners and investors can be significantly simplified and made predictable, and the underpinning information more available and reliable with the help of e-government applications. Just having a portal for businesses with reliable information about business licensing and permits can go a long way toward improving transparency and predictability, and the overall business climate. A review of the 2007 scorecards of municipalities in the above pilot indicated that those with one-stop-shop portals scored the highest.

Source: Hanna 2010.

be supported by applications to provide access to information on policies and regulations for investors. These applications are designed to improve access to business development information and extension and business support services. They are also used to facilitate access to key applications such as providing online legal and regulatory information services; improving SMEs' access to information on administrative requirements and business-related legal and regulatory frameworks; simplifying the initial search for items such as trademarks and patents; and providing firm-level support to SMEs such as advisory services, consulting, and so on.

Online government support services to businesses comprise of providing firm-level support to local SMEs and addressing the common issue of limited business and management skills among entrepreneurs. The IFC-supported online SME toolkits may be used as a starting point and/ or inspiration for such a portal. These include a number of how-to guides and articles in seven categories: accounting and finance, business planning, human resources, legal and insurance, marketing and sales, operations, and technology. The government's business support agencies can also host online business advisory services provided by various private sector experts. Clients can choose an adviser from among a number of business consultants and other advisers registered with the center and can expect to get a response from the selected expert within a short period of time. Conceivably, the delivery of such services can be made through mobile platforms. With the involvement of business and professional associations, DFGG measures can be strengthened and integrated into these ICT-enabled government-to-business transactions and support systems.

One critical area for public services improvement in developing countries is the *agricultural extension services*. One interesting application is the use of mobile phones to collect data on extension services and verify agents' visits. Simple mobile phones can be used as means of collecting both farmer- and agent-level data, thereby improving the accountability of extension services. Voice calls and SMS between farmers and extension agents can be used to collect data on the use of new technologies, costs, and yields on a more frequent basis, rather than waiting for annual agricultural surveys, when recall data on costs and production are often subject to measurement error. In addition, mobile phones can be used to verify agents' visits. Both of these applications could improve the monitoring and accountability of extension systems.

A third area is the delivery of *financial services to SMEs*, particularly via mobile phone. The financial sector is a leading adopter and enabler of e-business. It is a leading and intensive user in its own right—reaping major productivity gains and service improvements. Internet-based banking or e-banking and e-payments are becoming a delivery channel as they make it possible to dramatically decrease the unit costs of financial operations at the wholesale and retail levels.

Small, medium, and micro enterprises in developing countries are still largely excluded from formal financial intermediation. This is a long-standing development issue. It is being addressed by introducing e-finance, among others. Making e-banking and e-payments simpler and more affordable remains a major challenge, particularly for SMEs and the "unbanked." Relatively new players such as mobile-phone operators, e-payment technology vendors, and nonbank transfer operators are developing value-added operations via cooperative arrangements with the main players. One important role of e-payment is the small-scale financial transfer of migrant remittances. E-payment applications are increasingly relying on online mobile money transfer systems.

Mobile money does just two things: it vastly reduces the costs of the transfer of funds, particularly across distances, and also reduces the cost of the storage of funds. Like the ICT revolution as a whole, mobile money reduces the importance of physical distance, thus integrating millions of poor people and small businesses into the modern economy. It seems to be doing so in Kenya with M-Pesa, which has a 40 percent penetration among the poorest 20 percent of Kenyans. M-Pesa is a major success story of using mobile money transfers for all kinds of banking services (and payments for all kinds of public and private services) for the currently "unbankable" (Box 3.7).

A final broad area of using digital technologies to improve business environment and government-to-business services is to make information on *legal and regulatory issues* accessible to businesses, citizens, and NGOs— improving the business environment while protecting the public good. For example, to improve access to vital legal information for businesses, a web-based information service can be designed to cover issues of administrative requirements and business-related legal and regulatory frameworks. This web service could also include sections on important judicial opinions in business-related cases, draft laws and regulations, adopted laws and regulations, government directory/organization charts (with citations to laws), and frequently asked questions. The site could have information in an easily accessible form with a problem-solving, "how-to" focus. For example, it could explain legal requirements on how to start a business, initiate export/import operations, and so on. Conceivably, access to this information can be made available on the growing platform of mobile phones.

Mobile-based applications are used to enable citizens and social intermediaries to participate in holding corporations accountable and *monitoring government enforcement of regulations*. They are used for greater participation to bolster the monitoring and enforcement capabilities of weak or overextended agencies. For example, in Manila, individuals are using mobile phones and mobile text messaging to report vehicles they see emitting excessive pollution to a central database called *Smokebelchers Watchdog*. An environmental group leading the effort compiles a list of vehicles with five or more complaints against them and sends it to the land transportation office.

Not only can citizens and other stakeholders help monitor and enforce the rules set by governments, they can also promulgate bottom-up regulatory systems to address issues ranging from climate change to

Box 3.7

M-Pesa (Mobile-Based Money Transaction Service)

The mobile money transfer system M-Pesa has proved to be specifically applicable to the Kenyan market and context. In terms of number of users and transactions, M-Pesa is probably the biggest success story in mobile applications in Sub-Saharan Africa. It all started in 2005 when the Kenyan mobile operator Safaricom together with Vodafone realized the huge opportunity in airtime transfers and m-transactions (mobile transactions), and started a Department for International Development (DFID)–funded pilot mobile payment service later named M-Pesa. Since its launch in March 2007, the uptake of M-Pesa has been very impressive, and the number of agents and subscribers has grown exponentially.

Within the first 9 months after its launch, M-Pesa announced a subscription base of a million users and almost 1,400 agents operating across the country. In January 2010 M-Pesa had registered more than 9 million customers and there were 17,000 M-Pesa agents in the network.

The size of Safaricom (critical mass of subscribers and a majority market share), the composition of the management team (collaborative knowledge), the regulatory dispensation, and the need of the subscribers (urban-rural remittances were already taking place) all contributed to its success.

M-Pesa can be used by anyone with access to a mobile phone and subscribed to the Safaricom network; all that is needed is an authorization, transaction code, and proof of identity. Safaricom has been using the M-Pesa system as a loyalty product to retain and acquire new customers. Beyond money transactions, M-Pesa is now being used in various other ways. Some of the notable forms of usage include saving money, paying bills, buying goods, and buying airtime. The unintended usage of M-Pesa has been innovative, forming a basis for developing new services by Safaricom. For example, it is common to get public transport users to pay via M-Pesa whenever cash is not enough. Safaricom picked this usage to develop a mechanism for travelers to pay for their bus tickets via M-Pesa.

Safaricom has now partnered with almost 100 organizations who accept payments using M-Pesa, ranging from banks, media houses, government agencies, microfinance institutions (MFIs), and insurance companies. Each of the organizations has a unique number that customers enter before specifying their bill number. There is evidence that many other organizations accept payments using M-Pesa informally as well.

An innovative usage of M-Pesa can be found in a project run by Grundfos LIFELINK, a subsidiary of the Danish water pump manufacturer Grundfos. LIFELINK is building automatic, solar-powered wells and to sustain and maintain these wells, Grundfos and Safaricom have developed a pay-per-use system. The system allows clients to purchase water credits via their M-Pesa account into a Grundfos M-Pesa business account under the "Pay Bill" functionality. The credit is then loaded onto the client's smart card. Once inserted "into a slot on the tapping point, the water automatically starts running until the card is removed and the amount corresponding to the amount of water tapped is deducted from the card" (Safaricom 2009).

In terms of improving financial access in Kenya, M-Pesa's impact is significantly visible. A survey by FinAccess in 2009 showed that the use of services from nonbank financial institutions had grown from 8 percent to 18 percent since 2006. This cumulatively contributed to an increase in those who are financially included from 26 percent to 41 percent. M-Pesa also contributed to a significant growth of remittances within Kenya to 52 percent in 2009 compared to 17 percent in 2006 (FinAccess 2009).

The latest numbers on M-Pesa users in Kenya suggest the huge potential impact of this application for serving the poor and developing grassroots businesses. Based on overall subscription growth rates, it was projected that by the end of 2010, 4 out of 10 of the poorest 20 percent of Kenyans will have used mobile money, along with more than 90 percent of those in the top two quintiles.

Source: Hellström 2010, and author.

corruption to labor conditions in the overseas factories that manufacture garments for Western consumers. *CorpWatch.org*, a San Francisco–based nonprofit, established an array of analytic tools that empowers amateur corporate investigators (and social intermediaries) to monitor corporate abuses. The Cocoa Initiative, a multistakeholder effort to eradicate child slavery from the cocoa supply chain, helped initiate dialogue to establish mutually agreed standards for corporate conduct. Now, NGOs, labor unions, cocoa processors, and major chocolate brands are developing a transparent certification process for cocoa suppliers that do not rely on forced labor. The initiative fosters community-level actions that change the way cocoa is grown.

As globalization and interdependence intensify, transparency-based regulatory solutions have taken hold in some countries. Other domains where nascent models of participatory regulation are taking hold include: forest management, extractive industries, workplace health and safety, environmental regulation, tax evasion, and other abuses. ICT tools are often necessary to monitor and enforce regulation, to mobilize citizens and social intermediaries to make government-to-business transactions transparent, and to mobilize local businesses as key drivers for effective and accountable government. Yet, applying ICT to strengthen DFGG in the regulation and service of businesses remains a neglected area in developing countries.

Political Accountability

In addition to monitoring and enhancing the transparency of elections, ICT may be used to monitor the behavior of officials and improve parliamentary processes in many ways—improving transparency and openness; providing universal access to citizens; improving the mechanisms of accountability of legislators to their electorates; enabling dialogue between the parliament, its members, and the citizenry; and facilitating deliberation and legislative decision making.

Some *parliamentary* websites are intended to inform and engage the public; others are intended to facilitate the internal decision-making processes of the parliaments. The former type includes projects that disseminate information on proposed legislation and the legislative process, committees and members, parliamentary calendars, and transcripts and other materials from hearings or debates. Systems aimed at parliamentarians themselves may include online notices and voting. An example of a website that contains both features is the site of India's Council of States (http://rajyasabha.nic.in). The website for South Africa's Parliament (http://www.parliament.gov.za) also includes a range of information for both the public and MPs.[4] The Mzalendo website keeps an eye on the Parliament in Kenya, and uses ICT to promote interactions between citizens and MPs.

A UN World e-Parliament Report concludes that there is a significant gap between what is currently possible with ICT and what has actually been accomplished (UN 2008). There is increasing pressure on parliaments to be transparent to ensure that their activities are recorded and accessible to civil society and citizens. As the Internet has become increasingly important for the informed participation of citizens, parliaments must be committed to bridging the digital divide and ensuring that their decisions can be understood and analyzed by their constituents. The crisis of legitimacy of parliaments is ascribed to their inability to safeguard the diversity of the interests of the communities they represent. Traditional practices of parliaments in developing countries, including deliberations and document processing, are highly inefficient and slow and can be significantly enhanced with modern communications and the intelligent use of ICT. Moreover, many challenging issues facing parliaments are global problems or have global implications and can benefit from timely access to global knowledge, and the actions taken by other legislative bodies.

ICT offers opportunities for parliaments to reach out to the public and provide an accounting of parliament and legislators' actions—attendance, voting records, codes of conduct, performance, and integrity. Moreover, in view of a declining involvement of citizens in public affairs, modern technologies have raised the prospects of reengagement in the democratic process.[5] Progressive legislators can use social networking tools such as blogs and wikis to force the executive branch to account

---

[4] See also examples from the United Kingdom and United States: http://www.data. gov/ and http://transparency.number10.gov.uk/#.

[5] As in the 2008 U.S. presidential elections.

for various expenditures and to engage their constituents in timely consultations and feedback. As parliaments become more visible through the web, privacy and security issues become critical to ensure the integrity of parliamentary transparency and the confidentiality of citizen communication.

Monitoring elections is another key application area. Having transparent and credible elections is a key to political development and trust in government. Ushahidi ("witness" or "testimony" in Swahili) developed a crowdsourcing information- and Internet-based mapping site that allowed users to submit eyewitness accounts of election fraud and riots via e-mail, text, or Twitter. It is one of many examples of tools that empower millions of ordinary individuals to play a larger role in development, from democratic decision making to crisis management, to protecting public health (Tapscott and Williams 2010). Ushahidi achieved broad-based participation. It is now used by many civil society groups around the world. Crowdsourcing has proven to be particularly useful in volatile situations where citizens may be able to provide quick geo-referenced information to mobilize help (Box 3.8).

Social networking tools are influencing the politics of the African continent in key political contests. In Nigeria leaders rapidly came to terms with the political significance of new forms of communication and networking sites, such as Facebook and Twitter, as the country went to polls in 2011. Politicians were quick to learn that the combination of demographics and access to ICTs required new strategies for communicating with their electorate: the president declared his intention to run for the presidency on Facebook, other politicians also adopted the site as a campaigning tool; the Lagos state governor, and many other state governors, established a campaign presence on the social networking site.

Technology is also playing an important role in making voters aware of elections and encouraging transparency. The Independent National Electoral Commission (INEC) has deployed 240,000 people and 132,000 data capture machines to help with registering voters in what has been described as "Africa's single largest technology project ever." And Reclaim Naija, a broad-based platform for promoting transparency, launched a website using Ushahidi, the software developed in

Box 3.8

Ushahidi: Crowdsourcing Data from Citizens on Elections and Crisis Situations

Ushahidi maps incidents through crowdsourcing data to generate quick information that complements data from official monitors, raises awareness of certain incidents, and helps to mobilize support for preventing or mitigating any crisis situation. The platform first emerged during the 2007 Kenyan presidential elections, and was later deployed in countries ranging from Afghanistan to Haiti. Outside of a crisis, this technology and methodology can be utilized to gather information from a larger sample of the population to increase government accountability as well as for project monitoring and supervision.

The challenges that Ushahidi addresses include how to gather information more rapidly from the field, learn about the experiences of citizens regarding a particular event or project, and track developments on the ground through visually recoding data on a map. The violence that erupted following the 2007 Kenyan elections prompted Ory Okollah, a Kenyan-born attorney and activist, to mobilize a team of seven bloggers and contributors to collect information from citizens on events happening on the ground and make it public. Their aim was to raise awareness of the incidents that occurred and complement information from official media outlets.

In its original conception, Ushahidi was a Web-based tool built to collect information directly from citizens—otherwise known as crowdsourcing. The citizens can send in information in an SMS to the Ushahidi short code or through new media, which is then mapped for the public to view online. Between December 30, 2007, and April 1, 2008, the platform had 45,000 unique visits, 173,000 page views, and 220 incident reports from 131 unique contributors. Citizens entered crisis information regarding specific locales. In addition, they added firsthand reports and pictures that were not being reported by official sources.

Ushahidi is nonprofit organization and is supported through grants from foundations such as the MacArthur Foundation, Omidyar

Network, and Knight Foundation as well as through contracting work to supplement these grants.

Ushahidi has achieved broad-based participation. Crowdsourcing has proven to be particularly useful in volatile situations where citizens may be able to provide quick information, which can then be verified and used to mobilize help. Mapping has provided historical records of citizens' experiences in a crisis. Key benefits include:

- Ushahidi reports document an important number of violent events not reported by the media.
- Many citizen bloggers used real-time updates sent to them via SMS, primarily from rural areas.
- Contrary to the news media, Ushahidi data always had specific location information.

The efforts to resolve the volatile postelection situation benefitted from having multiple sources of information on incidents occurring in all parts of the country. Reports via SMS gave citizens, even in rural areas, an avenue to be heard and to express what is going on in their community. The visual aspects of map mashups and timelines make it possible for readers to visualize the crisis when they see the chronology, hotspots, and indications of interventions in one map, thus getting a bigger picture of what is going on and learning how to help during a crisis.

Three key challenges face further deployment of this popular platform:

- *Availability.* The need for offline data sync in case of poor Internet connectivity.
- *Usability.* The need for speech-to-text recognition to mobilize illiterate citizens.
- *Capacity.* The need to build relationships with partners to increase the number of administrators for scale.

Source: World Bank.

Kenya to monitor electoral violence. The likely long-term effect of all this is difficult to predict. What is hoped for, however, is that it will bring about a significant change to the nature of democracy and political campaigning in Nigeria.

Monitoring officials. The monitoring of democratic functions is also relevant outside elections. In Brazil, for instance, the application *Adote Um Vereador* ("adopt a councilor") provides a wiki-platform to encourage citizens to adopt local politicians, follow their work, and blog about their observations, thus giving the electorate better influence over the local politicians they elect. Similar platforms are used to observe municipal councils in other countries.[6]

Policy-making institutions in Africa and elsewhere remain constrained by lack of access to timely information, and limited capabilities for policy analysis, data mining, information sharing, and knowledge management. Many e-government applications can help improve public strategic management, policy making, and the management of knowledge resources. Information in support of oversight and policy making in developing countries is scarce, dated, and unreliable, with the following serious consequences (Hanna 1991; 2010):

- Lack of evidence-based policy making and planning without facts or monitoring of impacts
- Poor public financial oversight and risk management
- Cumbersome data collection and fragmented reporting systems combined with overload of unprocessed data
- Underdeveloped monitoring and evaluation (M&E) systems
- Poor decision support systems at all levels of public management

Similarly, communication systems in support of policy making suffer from:

- Poor horizontal communication across sectors
- Slow vertical communications among levels of decision making
- Unreliable feedback from beneficiaries

---

[6] http://transperency.globalvoiceonline.org.

- Underdeveloped networks among stakeholders
- Limited exchange of local development experience
- Isolation of think-tanks from providing timely inputs toward policy making

Fortunately, advances in ICTs are permitting the use of mobile devices to survey and collect data relatively quickly. Also, analytics or business intelligence tools provide a quantum leap in capturing and analyzing masses of information for policy making and strategic management. Areas of applications range from e-Cabinet and e-Parliament document management and decision support systems to modernizing national statistical systems. Analytics can be applied to government call centers and citizens' complaints, for example, to detect patterns of service delivery problems, performances, and trends. The potential of using analytics for oversight, governance, and improved policy making for public services is huge and largely untapped. Complementary investments will be required in developing the analytical capabilities of policy-making institutions to realize this potential.

Improving Governance for Service Delivery

Information technologies can help improve governance and strengthen demand for effective public services via four channels, with varying impacts (World Bank 2016):

- Informing and identifying citizens so that citizens can access important services, and make the right decisions about selecting these services.
- Redesigning and automating processes to reduce opportunities for rent seeking and resource leakage.
- Increasing feedback from service users to track satisfaction, identify problems, and improve quality.
- Monitoring service providers to improve their management and accountability.

Digital technologies are having varying impacts across these four channels. The highest measurable impact is when lack of information and communication is the main barrier to overcome. This includes citizens' lack of knowledge about issues that affect their welfare and their inability to communicate with each other and with government, and government's inability to be informed about citizens.

One of the successful examples in developing countries is the use of mobile phones by citizens (including the poor in remote areas) to deliver relevant information that helped people make better decisions on their own welfare. Initial results from pilots in South Africa and Tanzania, suggest that regular SMS communication can induce behavior changes in expectant mothers by providing information on neonatal health (Agarwal and Labrique 2014). Initial promising results also come from m-health initiatives that assist health providers in recording patient information, in monitoring pregnancies, and in reporting drug stock-outs (World Bank 2012).

More recently, digital identification has given poor citizens a verifiable identity and enabled them to access services previously denied to them. Safety net programs are becoming much more effective through digital systems for registering, authenticating, and paying beneficiaries and promoting inclusion. For example, South Africa's welfare payment card relies on a debit card payment mechanism linked to a management information system and biometric identity database. Once beneficiaries register, a biometric debit card is issued in a few days, and the system automatically credits cardholder accounts monthly with the appropriate grant amount. India's digital identification program extends a nationwide infrastructure for service delivery to over one billion people.

Redesigning and automating processes, the second channel enabled by digital technologies, can be used to eliminate routine activities prone to error and manipulation, reduce the number of intermediaries in a transaction, and establish audit trail to curtail leakage and rent seeking. Most countries are focusing on redesigning and automating the mobilization and management of resources: budget preparation and control, tax and customs administration, government procurement, and management information systems for health, education, land management, business services, and social protection services. Kenya, Uganda, Mozambique, and South Africa, among other African countries, have streamlined services through one-stop computerized service centers that enable citizens and businesses to access a broad range of public services from multiple government departments at one location—expanding options, speeding delivery, and reducing opportunities for corruption.

To have significant impact, *automation of services must be accompanied by changes as may be needed in laws and management practices, business process redesign and simplification, regulatory and administrative reforms, and capacity building* for system users and managers. South Africa's tax modernization reforms, which began in 2007, coupled the technology investments with simplifying the tax code and reforming business processes in the tax authority. Revenue targets became a compulsory feature of managers' performance scorecards. Online tax filing increased from 40,000 individual tax return in 2006 to more than two million in 2009, with significant reduction in tax compliance costs (Yilmaz and Coolidge 2013).

Increasing user feedback and participation, the third channel, can be a catalyst for governance and service improvements. The private sector discovered the power of customer relationship management for more than a decade, and governments have recently followed suit, particularly in the cities of developed countries. Given the considerable inefficiencies in public sector delivery in developing countries the gains from embedding digitally enabled feedback in public management are potentially high. However, two conditions are required for user feedback to have impact: citizens must have an incentive to provide feedback, specific and actionable, and the service provider must have the incentive and capacity to respond and resolve the complaint (World Bank 2016). Government responsiveness can further motivate citizens to complain, creating a virtuous circle of feedback and responsiveness. A highly successful example of effective user feedback is the MajiVoice, the complaint mechanism in the Nairobi water and sewerage company (Box 3.9).

Complaints via general citizen feedback portals are less likely to be actionable and more likely to be disproportionately used by richer educated, urbanite, and more digitally literate individuals. This can potentially bias government responses. Government-initiated feedback can overcome such biases in citizen reporting and be more targeted at acquiring actionable information. For example, in Pakistan, under a Punjab Citizen Feedback Model, service providers record citizens' mobile numbers and a government call center sends SMS and voice calls to pubic service users to

Box 3.9

MajiVoice for Nairobi Water Company

Household water supply is an example of private goods that citizens use and have an incentive to monitor, and the responsibility for delivering the service lies clearly with a particular entity. MajiVoice is such a complaint mechanism in the Nairobi water and sewage company. Given the limited Internet use in the country, customers initiate complaints in person in person or through phone calls to the utility, generating a ticket number for tracking for both the customer and the utility. The customer receives an SMS message from the utility when the complaint is registered on a dashboard, and another when it is resolved. The dashboard enables management to categorize the complaint, delegate the issue to a specific staff, and track resolution. The dashboard enables the utility regulator to track performance.

The initial results have been impressive. Prior to MajiVoice, the Nairobi water company received on average 400 complaints a month. Since 2013, when MajiVoice was launched, the utility has been getting about 3,000 complaints a month, resolution rates climbed from 46 percent to 94 percent, and time to resolution dropped by 90 percent.

Source: World Bank 2015.

make targeted inquiries about satisfaction with 16 services with the data logged and tracked on dashboards (Bhatti, Kusek, and Verheijen 2015).

Monitoring service provider management is the fourth channel to improving governance for service provision. The incentive and ability of providers and managers to respond citizens depends on strong relationships of accountability between policy makers and providers. Digital technologies can strengthen such accountability within government through better monitoring of workers and facilities and through better organization and performance management. This is particularly critical in sectors like education, health, and agricultural services in Africa. The absenteeism of teachers, doctors, nurses, and agricultural extension workers is pervasive in developing countries, reaching a quarter or a third. Physical monitoring of providers is costly, particularly in rural areas, and the monitors are just as likely to shirk as the providers. A cost-effective solution is to use mobile phones to record attendance (using photos or thumb prints for evidence), and transmit data to a central database to generate monitoring reports.

Evidence from developing countries, shows that such digital monitoring can reduce absenteeism, but the technology on its own is not sufficient for government providers, who are difficult to dismiss or discipline (Aker and Ksoll 2015). *Technology has to be complemented by good management.* In Uganda, only combining teacher incentive pay with monitoring technology has reduced absenteeism. Also, reducing absenteeism is not sufficient to ensure that doctors, teachers, and administrators, once they show up, are motivated to serve the public well. Structural reforms in incentives, civil service, and accountability relationships are necessary complements to digitally enabled performance monitoring to make any fundamental difference in the way government bureaucracies are managed. Much more time and experience is needed to improve and scale up current efforts, even in OECD countries (World Bank 2016).

Phasing Transparency into Service Delivery

Having information on the availability and delivery of effective education, health, water, and other essential services is essential to transparency, accountability, and trust in government as well as citizen participation in problem solving and innovation to improve service delivery. Initial steps would aim to make key information on basic service delivery policies, entitlements, budgets, and performance meaningfully accessible to all citizens. In developing countries, most citizens do not know of their basic entitlements and performance. Citizens are therefore unable to benefit from their entitlements and play their roles. The lack of information also makes it easier for local officials and service providers to divert resources for illicit gain.

But achieving transparency is a long-term journey that should be phased in gradually and persistently. According to the Open Government Partnership (OGP) initiative, during the initial phase, governments should make available information on citizen entitlements, responsibilities, funds released, and actual performance levels related to basic services. The commitment should be specific: for example, at least 80 percent of all citizens will be easily able to access this information. The information should be disaggregated to the lowest level (for example, x and y services are free for pregnant women, z dollars per student will be sent to each school per student) and presented in a user-friendly (visual) manner so as to be relevant and meaningful to ordinary people. The "retail" popularization of information can often be best done by professional communication companies or CSOs; therefore, governments should make such information (in raw data) available to these third parties and foster its dissemination to the lowest levels, including through radio, TV, Internet (Facebook), and mobile-phone platforms. Governments should commit to post information on public notice boards at all public schools, dispensaries, water points, libraries, and local government offices. Governments should foster easy feedback mechanisms and provide cooperation to independent monitoring efforts that seek to assess the reach and quality (meaningfulness, value) of the public dissemination of information, and commit to specify and take swift measures to remedy problems.

Many developing countries have started on this journey (Open Society Initiative 2011). Further steps recommended along the journey are described in Box 3.10.

Box 3.10

Further Steps for Informing Citizens about Service Delivery

Initial steps in providing information on service delivery involve making key information on basic service policies, entitlements, and performance accessible. The goal of more substantial steps would be to make key information on the execution of policies, *attainment of results*, and independent audits meaningfully accessible to all people and in a manner that allows comparisons. In many countries, the key challenge is not the need for better policies, but a better implementation of these policies and the translation of funding and inputs into meaningful results. Particular emphasis should be placed on two aspects—procurement and achievement of outcomes—because these areas tend to be rife with problems and/or tend to be neglected and can often enable tangible citizen engagement.

In the information they provide, governments should proactively disseminate and enable comparisons of different sorts (actual vs. policy;

this year vs. previous years, our school vs. other schools), because it is *in comparing that data achieve meaning*. Comparisons also allow citizens (and authorities) to more effectively compare performance, assess value for money, and exercise choice and accountability. Accordingly, governments should commit to tracking and making publicly accessible a specific set of (quantitative and qualitative) measures to assess execution of policies and attainment of progress. The underlying data used to assess progress should be made publicly available, in formats that can be easily processed by third parties. Information should be provided to the lowest disaggregated facility or community level (for example, school, health facility, village) and unit prices (per textbook, per water well constructed) so as to be meaningful and relevant to citizens. The information should be available on user-friendly, interactive online platforms that allow users to tailor searches and queries, and in particular make comparisons across timelines, geographies, and sectors, and against policy commitments. In particular, information from different sources should be presented side by side. Because computer-based Internet access, while growing, is still constrained in developing countries, explicit efforts should be made to make information available on public notice boards, on popular mobile-phone platforms, and to foster synergies with other mass media (for example, FM radio) and social intermediaries.

Finally, governments should foster easy feedback mechanisms and provide cooperation to truly independent monitoring efforts that seek to assess execution of public services and quantity/quality of attainment, and commit to specify and take swift measures to remedy problems. While ad-hoc monitoring as need arises can be helpful, it is now possible to establish systematic monitoring mechanisms that monitor what is happening at the lowest levels, and involve impartial academics and CSOs who produce credible "report cards" to the nation. Because the quality of underlying data used by governments can be uneven, independent monitoring should also assess reliability of data used. Some African countries have made such substantial steps: education public expenditure tracking surveys (Uganda and Tanzania), medical stock-outs (Ushahidi and Huduma in Kenya), and data searchable to facility level (Uganda).

The goal of the most ambitious steps would be for the government to foster civil society and direct citizen participation in information sharing, problem solving, innovation, and practical accountability so as to improve service delivery. The constituencies most affected by and often most knowledgeable about realities, constraints, and opportunities regarding service delivery are the millions of citizens and grassroots CSOs, and yet they are least consulted or involved in solving persistent service delivery challenges. Creating serious and practical opportunities for citizen involvement may provide a huge untapped reservoir of knowledge and goodwill, align incentives effectively, and create greater trust, which are all essential to solve service delivery challenges. New technologies and decreasing costs of communication, particularly the mobile phone and fast-growing social media platforms, enable unprecedented avenues for information sharing and demand-driven collaboration.

Accordingly, it is recommended that governments should establish a set of clear principles, regulations, and tools to foster an enabling open environment for multiple state and independent actors to engage and provide feedback and ideas. The key here is to set the conditions in which interested parties can access and generate information and ideas easily, undertake their own analyses and communication, innovate new tools (think apps), and help catalyze an exciting "ecosystem" of ideas and actions. The role of governments here would be to support third-party (or local government) bodies to facilitate such an environment, to encourage easier exchange and critique, to take feedback seriously and respond to it reliably, and to set incentives right within the government to tap into new ideas, experiment and rigorously evaluate them, and adopt them at scale. Funding and awards can be set up to spur innovations and problem solving so as to allow comparisons and to reward those in government who exercise bold leadership. Feedback mechanisms should be set up that are built around what people already use and like (for example, mobile phones, markets, schools) and multiple opportunities should be provided to cater to different groups and mitigate against some channels not working.

Source: Transparency and Accountability Initiative 2011.

CHAPTER 4

Political, Institutional and ICT Challenges

This chapter puts the various tools and applications of digital technologies into broader informational, public service, and sociopolitical contexts. The aim is to develop appreciation of the political, institutional, and technological challenges arising from these contextual settings in developing countries. Chapter 5 draws lessons and guidelines for policy makers and service providers to address these challenges. Chapter 4 proceeds as follows:

- First, we focus on the role of information for governing service delivery as both providers and consumers of services benefit from information flows that enable consumers to exercise influence on the quality of service, and also enable providers to offer better services and obtain timely feedback on their performance.
- Second, we map the range of actors that can be involved in strengthening Demand for Good Governance (DFGG), as DFGG initiatives genuinely gather momentum when they are built around a reform coalition that includes state and nonstate actors. We draw on research that shows how context shapes technological impact and the need to understand the incentives, capabilities, and strategies of the stakeholders and the sociopolitical context in which a technological intervention is meant to increase accountability.
- Finally, we identify key challenges that influence and condition the success and impact of information and communication technology for governance. The challenges are divided into two broad categories: those concerning the sociopolitical context for applying

ICT and social accountability tools, and challenges specific to the adoption and use of ICT in a developing country. Understanding the first category of challenges is essential to applying ICT tools in support of accountability and transparency measures.

This chapter focuses on the challenges and constraints to harnessing the power of ICT for service delivery and governance; but this focus should not discourage policy makers and service providers from managing these challenges and realizing the new opportunities. Governance and public service challenges are the core challenges of economic development. Digital technologies present perhaps the most promising means to meet these persistent challenges. Traditional, supply-driven approaches to strengthen governance and improve public service delivery must now deploy the new tools for effective governance and agile public service, deemed necessary to cope and thrive in the context of a twenty-first-century digital world.

Information, Service Delivery and Governance

Understanding the role of information in service delivery is necessary to improve services and deepen institutional reforms around governance, transparency, accountability, and participation. It is also critical for the effective application of ICT to improve both the demand for and supply of governance and innovation in public services. In first-generation public sector reforms in developing countries, the focus was on building institutional capacities, including capacities to forging new relationships between states, citizens, and markets. A second generation of public sector reforms is already under way, building on first-generation capacities, and focused on the delivery of public services in effective, responsive, transparent, and accountable ways. Institutions for service delivery are still weak in developing countries, primarily because of the slow pace of implementation of first-generation public sector and governance reforms. Service provision is politicized through capture by narrow interests, and is characterized by inefficiencies, corruption, and weak institutional capacity.

There is a growing recognition that limited information about the availability and quality of service inhibits service delivery and governance, and that second-generation reforms must improve information access and transparency of service delivery. Both providers and consumers of services benefit from information flows that enable consumers to exercise influence on the quality of services, while providers offer better services when these providers can obtain timely inputs on their performance. Similarly, there is growing recognition that information dissemination about the quality and availability of public services can assist in building trust, strengthening governance, and mobilizing demand and accountability for basic services.

Understanding the broader institutional environment for public services delivery serves is a key to improving the mechanisms for information that advances service performance and governance. Weak governance structures in developing countries underlie the persistence of institutional practices that constrain information flows and service delivery. These practices are legacies of centralization, weak participatory institutions, uncertain legal environments, and corruption. Citizens must still navigate the maze of regulations that cloud the operations of service agencies. Opacity perpetuates corruption. Moreover, the capacity of citizens to assert their interests and voices is important to service delivery. Apathetic and disengaged citizens and weakly organized pressure from below hamper the evolution of reciprocal links between service providers and recipients. Institutional reforms can unleash activists and civil society organizations (CSOs) who have created demand-driven constituencies for service provision. In turn, these constituencies would provide the long-term basis for additional reforms to reduce the governance gaps that prevent access to information and service delivery.

Similarly, mistrust of public institutions and service providers constrain effective service provision. Availability of accurate information about services and their costs helps build citizens' confidence and trust and reduces the gulf between recipients and service providers. Mistrust is also a legacy of bad performance records of public service provision and is worsened when citizens have little or no choice about the services that they receive, deepening the information asymmetries between providers and recipients. Disengaged citizens often lack organizational tools to contest their rights and demand information about services. This is a vicious circle. Information access is a necessary condition to rebuild trust in public services and to restore enduring reciprocity and accountability systems.

The impact of digital technology on citizen empowerment and government (and service provider) capability depends on the initial strengths of public institutions, and complementary investments in them. Effective adoption of digital technologies in organizations requires significant investments in new skills, changes in processes and working arrangements, and the adoption of new management and business practices. Policy makers and public administrators need to have the incentives to make these investments and to manage organizational change. Digital technologies, aligned with incentives of politicians, public administrators, and service providers can be highly effective in improving services. But patronage-based bureaucracies can resist change. Sustained collective action is often necessary to address service delivery failures and overcome these institutional constraints.

The impact of digital technology also varies by service (World Bank 2016). For services that are easy to monitor and based on routine tasks, digital technologies can improve outcome rapidly, even when institutions are weak, as with money transfer and licensing. But for services that are hard to monitor and require more discretion from workers, the quality of institutions is more important. In such cases, technology only augments the initial institutional conditions in areas such as teaching, and health services.

Some sectors such as health and education are dominated by technical information that is not readily accessible (understandable) for the public, posing challenges to communications, monitoring, and information sharing. Experts often fail to disseminate their messages to the larger public, perpetuating technical information gaps between providers and recipients of services. This is a common barrier to demand-driven services innovation that can be managed (but not fully overcome) through improved communication channels, clarity of information, visualization, and transparency. Information asymmetries can be significantly reduced by broadening the accessibility and reach of information about services, and by democratizing technical knowledge for easy access and dissemination. Countries that have embraced digital technologies in service delivery markedly improved service delivery and boosted accessibility. The new media, such as mobile phones, further strengthen the demand side of governance and accountability for public services by reducing information asymmetries and galvanizing citizen voices and action in service delivery.

The variation in interactions and interdependencies of digital technologies and institutions, by service and activity, combined with the diversity of institutions and sectors should be understood and used as a guide to policy, and investment planning for governing and improving service delivery. Such understanding of context can open many possibilities for improving governance and service delivery in even the most challenging environments in Africa.

As information empowers, the dilemma is whether its availability in the absence of adequate resources to deliver services would raise false expectations and exacerbate public disenchantment. In some cases, building a modern information system for service delivery may be more urgent than the narrower option of improving citizens' access to information about antiquated and dysfunctional services. Public–private partnerships (PPPs) are often prescribed in Africa and elsewhere to meet some of the shortfalls in service provision, while securing accountability. Ideally, ICT should be applied to improve the supply of services while simultaneously improving transparency and accountability to public managers and service consumers. Improvements in the technological base of service delivery should aim to promote both service delivery improvement (supply) and service governance (demand).

Technology, Stakeholders and Sociopolitical Contexts

A range of actors can be involved in strengthening DFGG for different levels of ICT intervention. Traditionally, DFGG has been associated only with the work of nongovernmental organizations (NGOs). But it is important to note that other nonexecutive actors such as the media, parliaments, local legislatures, judiciaries, academia, and the private sector are all relevant stakeholders. Moreover, the state executive itself can strengthen governance and delivery of services through efforts at more open and responsive public management. For instance, a state-run broadcasting corporation involved in disseminating information about public programs and budgets is clearly promoting DFGG. Likewise, complaints and grievance redress mechanisms in line agencies are also mediating demand.

Diverse executive and nonexecutive actors are stakeholders in the process of strengthening public services delivery and governance (see Figure 4.1). Experience has also shown that DFGG and service reform initiatives genuinely gather momentum when they are built around a reform coalition that includes not just one of these actors, but several, including (perhaps, most critically) reform champions within the state executive.

It is critical to understand the conditions necessary for effective ICT interventions that attempt to increase accountability through transparency strategies. Unlike the use of ICT to automate government processes and service provision, the outcome of ICT use in support of service accountability is highly dependent on the stakeholders and political context. This issue is critical in view of the tendency of ICT specialists to be technology driven, while those dealing with governance and public sector

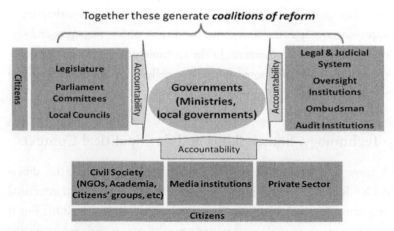

Figure 4.1 DFGG stakeholders include both executive and nonexecutive actors

Source: World Bank 2011a.

performance are often unaware of the potential of the new technologies to solve old and new service delivery problems. An accurate diagnosis of stakeholder context and the motivation of actors is critical to the success of technology for transparency interventions.

Research suggests three broad contextual categories for technological interventions that may be of general utility in guiding practitioners (Fung, Gilman, and Shkabatur 2010).

- The first category consists of technology-driven cases in which a technological intervention almost by itself produces increases in accountability as it unleashes latent desires by allowing individuals to take significant actions that were previously impossible with the technology being absent. This is a paradigm of technological determinism. Such "home-run" opportunities for technological intervention are rare and difficult to identify.
- The second and more common category consists of interventions that complement traditional public sector reforms and media efforts by making information about politicians, other officials, or governmental activities generally available. The success of these efforts depends upon the information collected being taken up by journalists or political campaigns and eventually made valuable and actionable to voters.
- The third and largest category consists of technological interventions that are tailored to advance the specific agendas of particular nongovernmental or governmental organizations by amplifying their capabilities and strategies, such as budget monitoring (Budget Tracking Tool in Brazil and Kenya) and election monitoring (Ushahidi in Kenya). In this category, success depends upon the successful marriage between particular technologies and the capabilities and efficacy of particular organizations that seek to utilize them. Most of the action in technology for accountability will lie in this third category, amplifying NGO and governmental strategies for accountability and public service improvement.

These findings suggest that practitioners should pay attention to four key questions about stakeholders and the institutional context in which a technological intervention is meant to increase public service performance and accountability:

- What are the *incentives* of potential users of the technology platform? For issues concerning public accountability, mass users often lack the incentives to acquire and act on information about corruption and malfeasance, or even about budget misallocations, whereas organized users such as journalists and reform-oriented NGOs may be highly motivated to acquire and act on this information.
- What are the *capabilities* of motivated users? Technological platforms should be tailored to the capabilities of potential users. Short message service (SMS) is better than the web when Internet penetration is low.
- Does an ICT intervention reinforce the *strategy* of potential users? Public agencies, CSOs, and NGOs deploy particular strategies, and some ICT intervention aimed to improve services and governance may or may not fit with them.
- Which *coalitions* are efficacious with respect to service performance and accountability problem? Progress requires an organization or coalition to possess the authority and resources to affect that problem. ICT helps when it is attached to such efficacious entities.

Sociopolitical Context

Understanding the sociopolitical context at a more fundamental level allows the designers of ICT interventions for service and governance improvements to take account of structural and political economy factors that might condition the selection and efficacy of these interventions. These factors may include wealth distribution, ethno-religious-linguistic divisions, literacy, political culture, checks and balance institutions, space for CSOs to operate independently, and so on. They condition how accountability is exercised in a country and can help explain public services failures and their sources, and thus guide them on how to correct this with DFGG and information and communication tools. Sociopolitical analysis can deepen our understanding of this context and guide the designers of DFGG and ICT in selecting, experimenting, and evaluating the interventions that are urgently needed.

Lacking such analytical tools, CSOs and governance practitioners have had to rely on piloting, experimenting, and drawing on in-depth local knowledge, while having limited capacity for scaling up or taking account of these structural constraints. For development agencies such as the international finance institutions, the risk is quite high to engage and scale up without such guiding tools or maps of the complex sociopolitical terrain. Alternatively, such agencies can add value by conducting a sociopolitical analysis of the context and thus provide knowledge and information on the nature of governance and public services challenges, political market failures, the channels for interventions, and ways to enhance coordination among local and external partners on such interventions.

But analytical tools for political economy assessments carried out at the macro level and often by external actors, cannot substitute for the in-depth local knowledge of specific contexts held by local actors. These tools and frameworks will have to be adapted to inform practitioners of how sociopolitical factors influence the scope for citizens and social intermediaries to interact with state agencies and service providers. Also, these tools are no substitute for piloting service reforms through local social intermediaries to test and discover local needs and accountability channels, capabilities, and constraints. These complementarities call for partnerships among economists, and social and political scientists, on the one hand, and CSOs and local social intermediaries on the other. Sector and ICT specialists can draw on this knowledge as they define key sector and service delivery outcomes and design interventions to strengthen client voice, accountability channels, and service supply response.

If accountability and reforms of public services are to succeed, the state must support the mechanisms to be used in exacting it (World Bank 2016; Blair 2011). Understanding and gaining government support is important to selecting particular service reforms and accountability mechanisms and enabling citizens to hold public officials accountable. The state can become a champion—as in the case of Porto Alegre, Brazil, where the mayor initiated a participatory budgeting process that engaged neighborhoods in determining municipal investment priorities, and where district delegates consolidate the budget and monitor its implementation.

The state can also play an active role by decentralizing state authority and bringing decision making and accountability closer to affected citizens. The state may also provide strong backing through ombudsman institutions, citizen review boards, statutory oversight institutions, and parliamentary committees with statutory authority.

Numerous accountability mechanisms rely on citizen activism, with the state playing a passive role. After elections, civil society and the media constitute the main vehicles through which citizens hold the state to account. Civil society requires acceptance by the state, however. The main "passive" role of the state is to be open and responsive to civil society's demands, to tolerate independent media, and assent to demonstrations.

Assessing the role of the state and its degree of support is important to selecting public services reforms and accountability mechanisms. Within the broad spectrum of social accountability mechanisms, the most important mechanisms—civil society, the media, and elections—are *not* those where state support is most active. They can be independent of state financing. They are critical to the sustainability of democratic governance and service improvement. They can be aided by various digital technology tools and, at the same time, they set conditions for the ICT role in strengthening citizens' feedback and service improvement mechanisms.

Mobilization of Public Opinion

Elections are the main accountability mechanism in representative democracies. While they may improve the delivery of public services and government's focus on the needs of the vast majority of citizens (Goetz and Jenkins 2005), they are not always a reliable means of making leaders accountable on specific issues. Representative systems for accountability must be combined with approaches to mobilize and organize the public to make sure that the people themselves can control the government. This involves deepening the dependence of government on the public, providing citizens with tools to monitor and sanction misrule. Citizens (and their social intermediaries) must develop capacity to sanction bad governance, and a minimum of free political space must exist to allow them to do so.

An organized public produces informed public opinion, and this has the power to change the incentives of public officials. How do you mobilize the public? The starting point is a realistic assessment of the contextual factors. Crucial to an open and inclusive public sphere are: guaranteed civil liberties, free media, access to official information and open government, a political culture of free debate, equal access to public areas, a vibrant civil society, and basic education. Social accountability tools work most effectively only where the context is open government and open society.

The presence of public demands for good governance is typically assumed, and the mechanisms that move people from inertia to mobilized opinion are left unexamined (Odugbemi and Lee 2011). Yet, accountability for public service performance requires the activation of public demands, and a constant monitoring and sanctioning of public sector functions from the bottom up. Clients of service provision, for example, must be informed about whether their needs and interests are being served. They must also have the requisite resources, perspectives, and channels to develop the ownership and collective efficacy needed to rise to action.

Mobilization is a process of moving individuals into collectives and transforming indifference into motivation and membership. This entails capacity building at three levels. At the individual level, this entails a transformation from being passive recipients of service provision and policy implementation to being active voices for service performance. This transformation is achieved not through information alone, but also through the discovery of shared values and the deployment of mobilizing frames and narratives—a key role for CSOs.

At the institutional level, capacity building entails building inter-organizational links between CSOs and government service-providing agencies. It entails constructing physical and virtual public spaces where information and interpretive frameworks are shared, practices are exchanged, and deliberative mechanisms are implemented. Again, this is a key role for CSOs and other social intermediaries.

At the mediating level of communicative networks, publics are kept informed of what government agencies are doing, and agencies are informed about gaps in service provision. This level entails the cultivation of civic education and mobilizing narratives as well as the socialization of watchfulness by the mass media, CSOs, government, and public.

ICT for Pro-poor Public Services and Governance

Three promising approaches to using ICT for pro-poor public services and governance can be adopted. The first is to embed ICT and transparency into poverty reduction programs. The second is to diagnose the ICT ecosystem and address all aspects that contribute to the digital divide in general and the use of social accountability mechanisms for the poor. The third is to gear e-government programs to serve the basic needs and priorities of the poor and the "common man." We illustrate these approaches in turn.

An example of embedding transparency into poverty reduction programs is India's National Rural Employment Guarantee Act (NREGA), a flagship antipoverty initiative. It contains an interlocking set of transparency provisions. These allow, for example, laborers who take part in this job creation program to access official records indicating the hours of work, payment of wages, and the sanctioning of projects. The recent development of a unique (biometric) identification system for over a billion citizens of India present a major leapfrogging in the use of digital technologies to deliver services and transfer resources to the poor while reducing leakage and increasing efficiency and transparency of various pro-poor social programs.

Many avenues can be pursued to ameliorate the digital divide facing the poor, and thus avoid having the digital divide create and reinforce an accountability divide. To start with, the fast penetration of mobile phones in developing countries has transformed their ICT ecosystem and created new channels for communication and access to applications. This should be leveraged to strengthen DFGG, and to the extent possible using open-source software applications such as Ushahidi. The Grameen village phone (http://en.wikipedia.org/wiki/Grameenphone) is a well-known example of deliberate use of ICT to improve gender equality; it demonstrates greater usage by women where women themselves are the ones to sell phone services, undertake outreach, and consultations with other women. This has also created a new livelihood and sense of empowerment for women in rural Bangladesh.

Telecenters (shared access to the Internet and ICT tools) can act as vibrant hubs for social innovation and empowerment. The experience of MSSRF (MS Swaminathan Research Foundation http://www.mssrf.org/) shows that individuals (particularly women) become empowered to operate outside of their traditional sphere of activity or to challenge collective social norms (Gerster and Zimmerman 2005). Adopting a community approach to ICT access is a cost-effective way for up-scaling, combining a multitude of services, facilitating the integration of traditional and new media, and providing a collective learning environment and social space for interactions (Hanna 2009; 2010). These information and communication centers expand user social networks, interconnect different ones, and connect local communities to large organizations. In some instances, these centers become a hub of social activism, a source of women empowerment (or protection from abuse), or a threat to the local elite. The United Nations Educational, Scientific and Cultural Organization's (UNESCO's) Community Multimedia Centers combine the Internet with other ICTs—the radio in particular, as community radio is most accessible to the illiterate and poor, and provides local solutions to local problems.

A pro-poor ICT environment would cover several fronts of policies and regulations. It would include promoting competition in ICT infrastructure provision, including last-mile connectivity. It would include least-cost and transparent subsidies to ensure access costs are affordable. It may include the use of voucher systems to promote private partnerships in subsidized public access provision to address the needs of the poor. It would promote the use of cost-effective and locally adaptable tools such as free/open-source software (FOSS), localization in local languages, and user participation in developing local content. Content is an often neglected element but remains the core element of any ICT ecosystem and is key to participation by the poor, and consequently should be adapted to the needs of the poor and rural areas. Information that is most critical to the poor can be given a priority in e-government programs, such as access to land records for farmers who needs these records to access credit and secure ownership. Pro-poor license obligations for service providers and operators may be appropriately included in the package. A pro-poor policy framework may also encourage community-based organizations and NGOs to adopt ICT into their operations, and to use these tools for pro-poor social mobilization. It would recognize and promote the special role of nonprofit community broadcasting for, by, and about the community (Gerster and Zimmerman 2005).

The third approach is to gear e-government programs to prioritize the core services that respond to the basic needs and priorities of the poor and the "common man." One of the promising examples is India's National e-Governance Plan (NeGP), subsequently renamed Digital India. It takes a holistic view of e-governance initiatives across the country, integrating them into a collective vision and comprehensive program. The NeGP aims to "make all Government services accessible to the common man in his locality, through common service delivery outlets, and ensure efficiency, transparency, and reliability of such services at affordable costs to realize the basic needs of the common man." However, implementation of this vision has been slower than expected, and the promised substantial impact is yet to be determined.

Political and Institutional Challenges

Applying ICT to public services improvement and governance means integrating ICT into a complex sociopolitical context. Emerging experience and research point to many political, social, and institutional challenges to applying ICT for service delivery and governance. Key among them are: poor understanding of context and impact, weak enabling policies and institutions, weak political commitment, limited public sector capacity for change management, limited civil society capacity for scaling-up and sustainability, and weak links among potential local partners and among e-government and sector specialists.

Poor Understanding of Context and Impact

The prevailing approaches to improving public service delivery and governance have mostly been "tool based" and rarely backed by proper diagnostics. In most cases, the use of DFGG has been driven by an interest to pilot specific tools (for example, scorecards) without actually diagnosing the operations to reveal what DFGG mechanism is needed and may be most effective in this specific context. Thus, there is a genuine risk of DFGG becoming a quick technical fix, rather than a well-thought-out response to improving the transparency, accountability, and participation in public service improvement on an institutionalized basis.

The same risk applies to the use of ICT, when focusing on specific technologies such as mobiles, the Internet, portal/websites, or specific applications of e-government, without diagnosing the context and appropriate technology that would fit the context and capabilities of users. In fact, technology-driven pitfalls dominate much of the evaluative literature.

The actual impact of various governance and ICT interventions at all levels—particularly of recent technologies and their impact at the micro (community) level—is insufficiently evaluated. This is expected in any new field of development practice. Lacking evaluative evidence, however, it is often difficult to access the merits of various options open for ICT-enabled interventions for transparency and service improvement. Even scarcer are assessments of errors of omission, of not leveraging ICT to supply adequate levels of information to citizens and service providers, and missed opportunities to address deficits in trust, transparency, and governance.

Weak Enabling Policies and Institutions

Social accountability depends largely on the extent to which civil society can enable communities to hold authorities and their representatives accountable for public services. Civil society organizations (CSOs) are essential actors in building a consensus for social and economic development. They can promote good governance by demanding consultation, representation, transparency, and accountability from authorities. And they are often uniquely positioned to advocate for community needs and to monitor delivery. An enabling environment is essential, and this in turn depends on favorable structural conditions. Factors typically associated with an enabling environment are: a legal and regulatory framework, political will, accessible government, and socioeconomic conditions of communities. In many developing countries, legislation is not designed to empower CSOs, and the legal mechanisms, judiciary, and police services are open to systemic abuse by the elites.

A related challenge is that governments often do not appropriately allocate and prioritize their pool of resources. Governments often do not prioritize resources for pro-accountability institutions (such as inspectors, controllers, and ombudsmen) as the value of these institutions is often less obvious than other departments such as ministries of health or education. These institutions' role is, however, of utmost importance in enhancing overall capacity to deliver services effectively to citizens through the promotion of good governance and accountability.

Pro-accountability institutions and mechanisms often do not have the necessary powers to enforce their recommendations. These institutions play a watchdog and advisory role but lack powers to hold officials accountable through legal procedures. This seriously hampers these institutions' ability to seek remedial actions on behalf of citizens who have suffered some form of injustice. ICT applications can strengthen their monitoring and advocacy roles, but cannot completely substitute for lack of enabling legislation and authorizing environment.

Weak Political Commitment

Political will is still lacking in many contexts across developing countries. Civil society groups are often intimidated by government officials and governments distrust civil society. Government officials also do not support the independent role of pro-accountability institutions. The key challenge for reformers and development practitioners is how to engender the necessary political commitment and adopt effective approaches to coalition building for DFGG and service improvement in various contexts. Investing in "independent" accountability institutions in the absence of true political commitment is unlikely to achieve transformational or sustainable results.

Limited Public Sector Capacity in Change Management

Open government faces many challenges—even in countries with advanced ICT infrastructure, a service culture, and active CSOs. Much of these challenges involve changes in values, attitudes, practices, skills, roles, and ultimately, leadership capacity for change management. Most civil servants and government agencies are still novices at using technology for encouraging participation and collaboration with citizens. Developing countries further lack the information culture and infrastructure to assure sharing, quality, timeliness, and securing of government data. The case of the U.S. Federal Government demonstrates encouraging results for a ready-to-open government, but also shows the successive challenges to be met in the journey toward openness, and some of the lessons that managing these challenges produce (Box 4.1).

Limited CSO Capacity for Scaling-Up and Sustainability

A lack of capacity to sustain and scale up social accountability initiatives is often faced by CSOs. These challenges are not just about having insufficient human and financial resources to build the capacity and scope of citizen-driven accountability interventions but also about not recognizing the nuances of these initiatives and adapting them appropriately to new contexts or social settings. Scaling up issues can be addressed through needs assessment, stakeholder analysis, education of end-users, and market analysis. Concern about sustainability demands developing innovative business plans, mobilizing various sources of funding, and creating an enabling ICT ecosystem, among others.

Box 4.1

Next Challenges for Open Government

The President of the United States issued a memo on his first full day in office calling for an "unprecedented level of openness in government" and subsequently, the Office of Management and Budget (OMB) released an "Open Government Directive" on December 8, 2009.

Open government outlines the following major steps: publishing government information online, improving the quality of information, institutionalizing a culture of openness, and creating an enabling policy framework. Since then, the sheer volume of data now available to citizens is unprecedented. The availability of new online tools has also encouraged certain citizens to participate more in government. But has the impact of such participation been substantial? Did open government create a more participatory or collaborative government? Did the government itself transform? It is probably too early to tell. But some challenges and lessons are emerging.

Transparency is one pillar of the Open Government Directive, and Data.gov is one key transparency effort. Within 7 months of its launch, it grew from 47 data sets to 118,000, all available on one Web site in open, machine-readable formats. The Directive required agencies to publish three "high-value" data sets that were available online in open format within 45 days. For each data set, Internet users can rate the usefulness of data, submit comments, and submit requests for other specific data sets. Another important transparency initiative is Web sites to track total government spending (USASpending.gov) and to track federal spending on information technology (IT). These Web sites provide dashboard-style interfaces that let citizens interact with key data and find out where their tax dollars are going, using geocoded data for all spending. These data sets are also put to use by third-party Web sites that have built tools around this data, and made them more usable.

Transparency has been the biggest success of the Open Government Directive. The next challenge is to put transparency into the transparency process, for example, agencies should be required to create a catalogue of all agency-owned data sets, so that citizens can better judge progress on releasing important data, and should share usage statistics, so as to show effectiveness and inform other users. Another challenge to further progress is the quality and timeliness of data. Online tools, such as expert forums could be provided so that user communities can assist each other in identifying problems in data sets. Policies may also limit the release of data related to national security and personal data, a reminder that government transparency depends not only on technology, but also on policy. Finally, there is the challenge of creating more transparency in the decision-making process itself, not just specific decisions after they have been made.

Participation is a second core value of the Open Government Directive—to identify the needs and tap the expertise of citizens. The U.S. government has started to use various tools to encourage public participation, from hosting online town hall meetings on YouTube, to collecting comments on government blogs, to using crowdsourcing platforms to collect ideas from the public on how to better fulfill agencies' mission.

While the opportunities for participation have expanded substantially, the response has been lackluster. A stronger response is more likely if the government demonstrates that it is listening. The strongest incentive to using a communication tool is how effective it is in getting across a message. Digital tools may be necessary for civil servants to extract meaningful information from the mass of electronic data they are likely to receive from public participation. Also, the government will have to show how the ideas submitted through such tools are being evaluated and which, if any, will be implemented. Online forums may provide opportunities for tech-savvy, politically motivated interest groups, but how can society be sure that all voices can be heard? Moreover, most government agencies are still novices at using technology for participation and collaboration. Most promising is the use of e-participation tools at the local government levels, where local officials can be more directly engaged with their citizens.

The third value of open government is collaboration—to make government more effective through participation between different levels of government and the private sector. The Obama administration has encouraged government agencies to use ICT to improve collaboration and use contests to encourage outsiders to participate. While these tools have not been applied extensively, they show promise. Governments may consider ways to advertise these initiatives more broadly, including partnering with the private sector to draw attention through popular Web sites. U.S. agencies still face collaboration challenges to share data, to report on data in common format to allow for comparison, and to jointly develop data privacy policies.

In conclusion, while the Open Government Directive has yet to create radical transformations in the U.S. government, its most important contribution may be nurturing a new culture of openness that embraces ICT.

Source: Adapted from Castro (2010).

Weak Partnerships among Local Stakeholders

Public sector managers often lack skills and experience in working with CSOs, to understand who they represent, and how they govern themselves and make decisions. On the other hand, CSOs need to be trained to work with the government and increase their knowledge of the policy process. Citizens (and their social intermediaries) as well as public service providers often lack mutual understanding. Development practitioners should learn how to not only bring these two parties together but also to allow them the opportunity to voice their grievances in a process that is mutually constructive. Social networking tools and continued communication can help build mutual trust and bridge cultural and information gaps between the two parties for improved governance and accountability.

Communication Gaps among Specialists (ICT, Sector and Governance)

Governance and public service reformers are often ignorant of the potential as well as the pitfalls of deploying ICT for transparency, accountability, and participation. They tend to view technology as a black box that works in isolation, or at the margin of governance interventions. On the other side, ICT specialists tend to ignore the context and motivations of stakeholders and hold the view that ICT, by itself, can automatically improve services and enhance transparency, accountability, and participation, regardless of service, institutional, and societal contexts. Thus, the communication gap persists between ICT specialists, on the one hand, and service providers, sector (e.g., health, education) practitioners and governance specialists, on the other, within governments. This gap continues to lead to missed opportunities and low payoffs from ICT investments in e-government, and from service improvement and governance interventions without ICT support.

The lack of such partnerships across disciplines is a major challenge to effective and sustainable service improvements. Many applications are developed by volunteer communities that get temporarily mobilized during a crisis but lack the strength to sustain these promising applications or take them to scale.

ICT Infrastructure and Ecosystem Challenges

This section briefly summarizes the conditions of the main elements of the ICT ecosystem in developing countries as they impact service delivery and governance: poor ICT infrastructure; filtering, censoring, and challenges to privacy; illiteracy; underdeveloped local content industry and unmaintained government websites; cost and affordability to application and content developers; and lack of sustainable business models for mobile apps for service delivery and accountability.

Poor ICT Infrastructure

Improved access to mobile telecommunications and the innovative use of mobile phones are promising developments for developing countries. There a range of promising initiatives looking at citizen-to-government accountability using mobile solutions. Many mobile applications have been rolled out and scaled up in health, agriculture, and finance sectors. However, mobile apps to improve transparency, accountability, and participation are still struggling for financial sustainability.

A major factor in the Africa region's low ICT adoption rates is the generally poor infrastructure. For example, according to World Bank, only 24 percent of Africa population have access to electricity (http://go.worldbank.org/8VI6E7MRU0). Areas that are connected to power grids often suffer outages, voltage spikes, and drops, and many countries operate under load-shedding agreements. It should be noted that for the consumer, having electricity access does not in itself equal actual use, as people might have access but still cannot afford it or have other priorities.

Limited network coverage and poor network quality still constitutes a challenge, especially in rural areas. Unreliable SMS deliverance due to increased traffic loads creates network bottlenecks and crippling SMS services. The existing documentation of network coverage and quality is not authoritative.

Filtering, Censoring and Privacy

Most developing countries view new technologies as a great possibility for social and economic development; some governments regard them as a threat and are therefore adopting new and multiple means for controlling these technologies. Technical filtering is the most known method but other tactics are emerging "such as the 'outsourcing of censorship' to private companies, the use of surveillance, and the manipulation of online conversations by undercover agents" (OpenNet Initiative 2009: 1). Filtering and censoring the Internet have proved to be a frustrating exercise for both governments and political activists. For example, in China, where enormous amounts of money have been spent to filter and censor the Chinese Internet, Chinese users still access and publish banned content. In Sub-Saharan Africa, even though many obstacles to access are infrastructural shortcomings rather than deliberate government policies, filtering and censoring are on the rise.

As Internet use continues to grow, laws regulating its use are being developed to encourage social and economic development. The legal and regulatory framework may also be designed in a way that restricts free expression. Once a government starts using filtering techniques originally intended for good purposes (to filter out child pornography, for example), nothing stops it from filtering whatever else is in its interest. Mobile-phone networks differ from the Internet in that they are centralized and therefore more easily controlled by governments.

Illiteracy

The success of M-Pesa indicates that technologically, textually, and numerically illiterate people find ways of getting the task done using mobile services—either by trial and error but more typically through mediated use (that is, by asking someone else to help with the task). Mediation usually involves a loss of anonymity and convenience, something that must be remembered when designing text-based services. People might know how to receive and read a message but do not know how to reply back, or are illiterate in the local language and cannot reply back.

Local Content and Government Websites

Rural communities are not just passive recipients of information, but content generators in their own right. The operators, third-party companies, and the government have an opportunity to capitalize on that—a chance to work with customers/citizens to deliver on their needs. The local content industry and its market are underdeveloped in most developing countries. Market research and development is needed to find out what customers/citizens need and to induce intermediaries and content developers to make innovations relevant to these needs.

The same applies to government websites which, rather than being citizen centric, tend to replicate government compartmentalization and fragmentation. They also tend to ignore content for the common man or social intermediaries. Websites are often static and their content is seldom updated. Once these websites are created, the question is often asked: does the government have a budget for website maintenance?

Sustainability and Affordability

The dramatic increase in mobile penetration may have inflated expectations about mobile apps for development, and diverted attention from the sustainability of these applications. How to develop affordable, sustainable applications and services for rural communities? How to create revenue for either cost-recovery or profit? These communities usually have low income levels, diverse indigenous languages, and low literacy rates. How to include illiterate mass populations who hardly have the means to access the Internet? And who should pay for the services— the government, the donors, the end user, a third party, or via public–private partnerships (PPPs)? Innovative PPPs are being experimented with throughout the developing world.

What is needed is an innovative business model that will (i) take away the cost for the end user, (ii) clearly save costs for the government or the service providers, and (iii) not depend on donor funding. Finding an innovative business model of this kind requires local research. Creating an "ICT fund for governance and public service innovation" at the national or global level may be necessary to help CSOs to partner with application developers to research, pilot, and replicate such promising business models.

For mobile phones to help development in poor countries, the technology must be affordable. Some research is pointing in the direction that mobile expenditure is diverting meager resources away from other critical needs of the poor. This impact on expenditure of the poor should be assessed to secure affordability.

Profitability of Apps for Social Accountability

Mobile communication is usually a highly competitive business-driven sector. If a nonprofit service is launched, it is usually being implemented as part of corporate social responsibility (CSR) programs in the entertainment, sports, housing, health, education, and environment sectors—sectors with maximum outreach, that are good for marketing purposes, and have few political hurdles. Public services governance, on the other hand, is a public good. Today, there are few innovative business plans that bring the two worlds together, and therefore social and governance applications end up low on the priority scale of operators. Further, public service improvement is a long-term commitment, with no quick fixes through a pilot or short-term intervention. There is, therefore, a good case for a government role to address market failures through PPPs with mobile operators, content developers, and civil society.

Mobile applications for social services and accountability are unlikely to be profitable and sustainable without donor support or government incentives, at least for application development and initial adoption. Programs to develop and diffuse such applications for DFGG must explore possible business models or search for sustainable sources for financing. Lessons can be drawn from applications for mobile money transfer. A survey by the Consultative Group to Assist the Poor (CGAP) suggests that profitability from M-Pesa (and other mobile-based money transactions) requires a long-term view, building on an existing voice communication base and on scaling up electronic transactions (Box 4.2).

Box 4.2

Business Models and the Sustainability of Mobile Money Transfers: The Case of M-Pesa

Mobile money contributions may be small compared to the current mobile network operator (MNO) total revenue, but they could be important for future revenue growth. Few operators will ever meet the high expectations they have for mobile money. Eighty percent of respondents to a survey expected mobile money to comprise 10 percent of total MNO revenue within 5 years of its launch. But for a number of MNOs, such as MTN Ghana, 10 percent of overall revenue easily exceeds their current nonvoice revenue from SMS and other services. It is highly unlikely any mobile money implementation is on track to meet these expectations of overall revenues within a 5-year time frame. This suggests recalibrating expectations.

For a number of MNOs, mobile money and mobile financial services may just be the single largest source of overall revenue growth. Some analysis done by AfricaNext shows that M-PESA's contribution to revenue growth exceeded 30 percent, even though its contribution to overall revenue was 10 percent. So, mobile money could be invaluable to future revenue especially when average revenues per user (ARPU) in voice continue to fall as mobile markets mature.

MNOs need to think long term about their role as a financial services and e-commerce providers in what is becoming an increasingly electronic commercial landscape in developing countries. MNOs could position themselves to be at the center of this landscape and in many markets, especially in Africa, they are in a very good position to do so.

Mobile money success is highly dependent on the existing size of the MNO's voice customer base. There is a belief among MNOs that mobile financial services can drive voice subscriber growth. In a number of markets, new entrants in the voice business or MNOs with small market shares have launched mobile financial services with that expectation. It is possible that mobile financial services may help retain customers, as it appears to have done for Safaricom in the face of increasing competition in the core voice business in Kenya. But offering financial services has not proven to be a source of subscriber growth. Customers of mobile financial services will come mainly from an MNO's existing voice base. The size of that voice base is even more critical if the strategy is to get to a critical mass of adoption in the wider payments market.

The implication is that in markets such as Senegal, Mali, Mexico, Niger, and, of course, Kenya, where a single MNO holds a dominant position, those MNOs are in a position to make the biggest land grab in mobile financial services. Where the voice customer base is fragmented, such as in Ivory Coast, Tanzania, or Brazil, the path to success is not clear cut. MNOs may consider improving their odds through strategic partners, which may involve working with each other. MNOs can build the road together—the mobile payments infrastructure—but then compete on the services that use that infrastructure.

There are three basic drivers of direct profit for mobile money. First, the obvious key driver of direct revenue is growth in active customers. In fact, high *inactive* customers mean that more transactions are expected from each *active* customer for the business to turn cash flow positive. In most cases, MNOs pay their technology platform providers on a per customer basis that, along with the upfront licensing fees, can add up to a grim picture when most customers are inactive. But it is not sufficient to have active customers. To see rapid growth in profits, MNOs need growth in transactions per month per active customers. Transactions per month per active customer for M-PESA Kenya may have more than doubled in 3 years.

Mobile money implementations are more likely to increase direct profit if their cost structure changes as the service grows. The cost structure should ideally turn from fixed marketing costs toward variable agent commission costs, which are costs that are directly tied to revenue generation from transactions. The study estimates that for M-PESA Kenya, the share of commissions paid by M-PESA to its agents in the overall cost structure must have gone from roughly 10 percent in year one to over 60 percent in year three.

The most significant driver is ultimately going to be electronic transactions per deposit ("electronic-only") because of a simple combined effect: less use per transaction of cash-in/cash-out at commission-based agents, which is the lowest margin-earning part of the business, and more use per transaction of the electronic platform, which is the highest margin-earning part of the business. It is estimated that M-PESA Kenya earns an estimated 18 percent weighted average gross margin on agent-based transactions compared with almost 100 percent gross margin on electronic-only transactions. M-PESA Kenya's "electronic-only" transactions grew 35 percent faster than agent transactions.

Growth in electronic transactions per deposit or cash-in presents a tantalizing outcome—less need for cash-handling agents over time, which is the most expensive and operationally the most challenging part of the business. But how do we drive more transactions per deposit? The answer is to have more electronic uses for the deposit. Even for M-PESA Kenya, the reason why we saw increasing transactions per deposit was not because people were sending domestic remittances to a wider range of recipients, but because they were doing other types of transactions. A large share of these other transactions was in fact small business merchant payments.

Source: CGAP blog by Kabir Kumar and Toru Mino.

CHAPTER 5

Guidelines for Policy Makers and Service Providers

How can ICT help enhance public services innovation and governance? How can ICT be used to strengthen third-party monitoring? What are the practical lessons learned from the emerging experience in Africa? What should be the guidelines and practices for policy makers and service providers in using ICT for governance, and public service improvement? What are the promising areas for future research and experimentation?

The proliferation of ICT is opening up government processes to a larger public, and is empowering ordinary citizens to demand accountability from their leaders. It is clear that new digital technologies can supply citizens and service providers with powerful tools for communication and mobilization. If used innovatively, they provide platforms where individuals can express dissent and offer solutions, thus strengthening participatory democracy and citizen-centric public service. For many developing countries this is a recent trend and the actual practice is far below the potential.

Investing in DFGG, aligning institutions and incentives within the governance ecosystem, learning by doing, prioritizing partnerships and knowledge sharing, doing research on best practices, and development of frameworks and analytical tools should all be part of the emerging lessons. They are taken into account in the following guidelines for policy makers, service providers, civil society organizations, and aid agencies. They are summarized in Table 5.1.

Table 5.1 Guidelines and Recommendations

What	How
1. Understand motivations and sociopolitical context	• Conduct context analysis to guide ICT-enabled service transformation and governance. • Make assumptions explicit regarding what information is needed for service innovation and governance, who provides it, who uses it, and its influence on behavior. • Understand motivations and capabilities of communities and social intermediaries. • Develop the governance policies and institutions that are complementary to ICT investments for good governance. • Understand incentives of citizens and service providers so as to create a virtuous cycle of feedback and responsiveness. • Strive for best fit, rather than best practice.
2. Build partnerships, capacity of grassroots partners, and government capacity to adopt participatory practices	• Build capacity of public sector and its partners for participatory practices, change management, social accountability, and customer relationship management. • Develop a strategic communication and outreach strategy, using media and localized knowledge services. • Practice partnerships across disciplines: ICT specialists, social development and public sector specialists, and governance specialists. • Promote partnerships among NGOs/CSOs, software developers, mobile operators, and government/service providers. • Enable rather than supplant bottom-up initiatives. • Adopt government procurement practices that support partnerships, transparency, accountability, and innovation to maximize public value.
3. Secure political commitment and leadership competencies	• Address e-government/e-service projects as socio-political-technical projects. • Secure political awareness and will, and build transformational and technical leaders competencies to engage citizens and manage open government social networks. • Use strategic communications and partnerships to nurture awareness and commitment. • Develop multilevel and multidisciplinary leadership. • Empower citizens to hold service providers accountable.
4. Adopt best practices in process and service automation	• Adopt a whole-of-government enterprisewide architecture and interoperability approach to e-government and e-service improvement. • Use e-government investments to integrate services across administrative and government layers

	• Adopt process transformation practices when putting public services online.
	• Mobilize demand and monitor adoption of e-services
	• Secure complementary changes in laws, regulations, and management practices.
	• Take account of initial institutional conditions, and of amenability of service to monitoring and citizen participation.
5. Deploy supply and demand measures synergistically	• Give attention to demand for governance and public service, not just supply.
	• Act on both supply and demand measures synergistically,
	• Use DFGG lens to prioritize investments in e-services and secure continuous improvement.
	• Sequence e-government and ICT for DFGG to facilitate openness and accountability from the start.
	• Adopt a phased approach to open government in line with capabilities and institutional learning.
6. Balance short- and long-term strategies for scaling up and sustainability	• Explore possibilities and preconditions for scaling up while initiating pilots.
	• Amplify local NGO and governmental strategies of accountability and service delivery.
	• Phase transparency into service delivery.
	• Counterbalance the incentives for short-term results within governments and their development partners.
	• Create an enabling environment for sustained progress by mobilizing public opinion (through traditional and new media), enacting Freedom of Information laws, organizing service user groups, and so on.
7. Address enabling environment and ecosystem of ICT sector	• Address systemic constraints: availability and cost of bandwidth, digital divide, interoperability, ICT skills, and change management skills, legal and regulatory environments, PPPs, and so on.
	• Nurture ecosystems that support mobile-phone networks, shared access centers, local content, and so on.
	• Develop ICT governance in public sector to support information sharing, government-process-reengineering, information sharing, privacy, and security.
	• Use ICT to build coalitions and partnerships for service innovation and accountability.
8. Integrate pro-poor policies into ICT-enabled governance and service improvements	• Diagnose sociopolitical context for pro-poor governance and service improvement.
	• Build capacity of pro-poor institutions to leverage ICT for public services.
	• Assess how the media can better augment DFGG on behalf of the poor.

Continued

Table 5.1 Guidelines and Recommendations (Continued)

What	How
	• Target key elements of the ICT ecosystem for pro-poor governance: taking a community approach for affordable access to ICT, developing local content in local languages, adopting free/open-source solutions (FOSS) in government and CSOs. • Liberalize licensing particularly for community radio, blend "old" ICTs with the latest, reduce the cost of access to mobile and the Internet for the poor, and so on. • Embed ICT for governance and service innovation into demand-driven poverty-reduction programs.
9. Conduct research, learn by doing, and capture and share best practices	• Emphasize monitoring and evaluation, to understand how the digital tools can be leveraged most effectively in different sociopolitical contexts. • Involve communities and promote South–South exchange and partnerships. • Move beyond few celebrated success stories. • Prioritize research on enabling policies and institutions. • Capture the tacit knowledge of users and communities as they experiment in different contexts.

Source: Author.

1. Understand Motivations and the Sociopolitical Context

   Conduct context analysis prior to guide ICT-enabled service innovation and governance. Context is absolutely crucial. There is no single 'silver bullet' or special recipe for creating successful social accountability initiatives. The best strategy will always depend on the social and political context. The choice of an appropriate approach will depend on whether there is an enabling or hindering environment in terms of whether the political regime is democratic, political and civil rights are guaranteed, there is a culture of political transparency, participatory mechanisms are institutionalized, or civil society and the government are strong (Claasen, Alpín-Lardiés, and Ayer 2010). Similarly, ICT approaches to promote good governance depend on the sociopolitical context; the adopted approach to social accountability; as well as on the state of ICT infrastructure, ICT awareness and literacy, and the enabling policies and institutions for information sharing, among others.

Make assumptions explicit regarding what information will be needed, who will provide it, who will use it, and how it will influence behavior. An accurate diagnosis of context and theory of action is critical to the success of technology for transparency and service delivery (Claasen, Alpín-Lardiés, and Ayer 2010). It is therefore important for those who support ICT-based transparency interventions to help tech entrepreneurs and activists by pressing them to lay out what their initial assessment of the context is, what information the ICT platform will provide and who will provide it, who will use that information and why, and how that use will result in gains for accountability and service improvement. Policy makers and service designers should include the whole universe of accountability interactions, and the implications of the proposed design on these interactions and on citizens and their social intermediaries. Periodically, they should revise their contextual assessment and theory of action and be ready to evolve in light of experience. ICT tools could improve the understanding and monitoring of context and stakeholders, and in turn, such understanding contributes to a more effective design and use of ICT tools for service innovation and governance.

Tailor the approach and focus of the intervention to the specific country context. At a macro level, more options are possible for ICT use for transparency in the context of open societies. This suggests a virtuous circle whereby democratization and public sector reforms (such as decentralization) can open up more channels for communication and ICT use for transparency and citizen empowerment. Some ICT applications, however, can initiate, further strengthen, and sustain more governance reforms.

Understand motivations and capabilities of communities, beneficiaries, social intermediaries, and service providers. These tasks would be especially challenging to aid agencies with little experience in engaging social intermediaries. Technology for transparency and public service improvement interventions, armed with ICT tools, frequently bypass such diagnosis and get "the theory of action" wrong. Such pitfalls are more likely when service designers are guided by a deterministic view of the technology. It should always be remembered that ICT applications for service transformation are not about technological innovation, but socio-technical innovation. This means at least equal attention to the social, political, economic, and institutional aspects of such innovations for improving governance and services.

2. Build Partnerships and Capacity to Deal with Participatory Innovations

Develop multistakeholder partnerships within the country. When developing ICT for accountability in public service, participants must recognize that this requires a partnership between the government, policy makers, regulators, network operators and service providers, hardware manufacturers, content providers, application developers, and civil society. Local capacity and local talents should be mobilized, new and old ICTs should be blended to cover the entire value chain, and the solutions should be demand driven. Good local content and relevant local applications are hard to find, especially content that fits the mobile-phone platform, which is the most personal service delivery platform of the future. At times, the media can be a necessary ally of civil society in increasing the pressure on governments and mobilizing public support behind specific governance and public service reform issues.

Assess capacity of local and national CSOs and build their capacity and networks in priority areas. CSOs' insufficient capacity to meaningfully participate in accountability mechanisms is common. Lobbying, social mobilization, and capacity building are essential. In almost all successful cases, champions were critical in giving support to the reform process. A capacity building program dedicated to practitioners in CSOs and in the government, would not only transfer skills but also enable practitioners to connect with others across developing countries. This capacity building should include capacity to identify opportunities to leverage ICT applications, new media, and ICT platforms for service transparency, accountability, and participation.

Enable, rather than supplant, bottom-up initiatives. By focusing on the enabling conditions and sectoral reforms, the government and its large development partners would complement and enable, rather than supplant or displace, bottom-up innovations and NGOs'

initiatives to develop ICT-based demand-driven measures for governance and service innovations. Aid agencies should be cautious in pursuing social accountability for services from the top or outside the country so as to move from donor-centered accountability to making governments accountable to their own citizens, and empowering local stakeholders to do so.

Broaden the interventions of development partners beyond the narrow focus on traditional counterparts in the government. Building partnerships and capacity among CSOs will demand from development partners to engage with a broad range of stakeholders and to pursue strategic communication and outreach strategy with those already active in DFGG and service inclusion. Development agencies are still narrowly focused on its traditional clients, often the central ministries. They need to engage with local governments, CSOs, the academia, and other actors in the DFGG arena. They should use ICT to invite the broader audience of stakeholders and partners to participate in creating solutions to the challenges of governance and service inclusion. They should also reach out to the media to enhance the impact of civil society on service delivery and DFGG. Aid agencies, international NGOs, and local think tanks also need to adapt and disseminate their knowledge services in ways that can be absorbed by local audiences and social intermediaries.

Build capacity for change management and the adoption of participatory and client relationship management innovations in public service. Giving citizens a voice requires a process of institutional change and capacity building to deal with open innovation. Often overlooked is the process of institutional change that must enable governments to be responsive to citizens. The benefits associated with participation— such as better and innovative delivery of public services—are only achieved when stakeholders are capable of and willing to deal with participatory innovations. The implementation of successful citizen participation initiatives involves a number of processes that are often ignored, such as the building of coalitions, and the crafting of suitable participatory processes.

Practice partnerships across disciplines concerned with governance, service design, management science, and ICT. Partnerships should bridge the disciplinary gaps between ICT specialists, public sector and governance specialists, social development specialists, and practitioners in priority sectors targeted for improvement. Those specialists often operate at different levels of government and are connected to different state and nonstate local actors, thus bringing different perspectives and understandings of the structural, social, and technical factors. The challenge of service transformation and governance calls for collaborative and multidisciplinary approaches. The promise of ICT for DFGG and for service delivery is unlikely to be fulfilled without strong partnerships across turfs and disciplines within government and aid agencies. Cross-sectoral partnerships would be necessary to meet this challenge, align ICT with strategies to promote DFGG, and scale up promising innovations.

3. Secure Political Commitment and Leadership Competencies

Recognize that e-government projects are socio-political-technical projects. In successful cases, political "will" was the key to proceeding with governance initiatives, and even a precondition to securing corrective actions by government officials and service providers. Using ICT for public services transformation is primarily a political project, and only secondarily a technical one. Both political commitment and technical leadership need to be developed for improving accountability of public services via ICT interventions.

Secure political will and technical leadership through awareness and new competencies. The imperative of securing political and technical leadership suggests a need to build leadership awareness and competencies to leverage ICT as an integral part of reforming governance and public service. E-government for transforming public services and open government requires transformational leaders and change champions within and outside the government. Public sector leaders and chief information officers must develop the necessary competencies to engage citizens, manage information resources, open government data systems, leverage social networks, and hone the competencies needed to integrate knowledge and skills from multiple participants, including social intermediaries. This should be combined with programs to heighten awareness of political leaders (and the public at large) of the opportunities open to mobilize demand and secure the supply of the technology for governance and socioeconomic transformation.

Political commitment should not be confused with slogans and public relations. E-government and open data initiatives are not magic bullets. Political commitment is to do what it takes to implement open government and make it accountable: time, political capital, and political fights. It means painful changes in roles and attitudes of civil servants, and leading by example to make these changes. It means power shifts and power sharing within government and with citizens and civil society. These changes call for transformative leaders at many levels of government. It also means building the necessary environment for experimentation and innovation.

4. Adopt Best Practices in Process and Service Automation

Adopt a whole-of-government enterprisewide architecture and interoperability approach. E-government offers substantial opportunities for sharing information and integrating services across administrative and government layers (Hanna 2016). To capture these opportunities, service providers and public administrators should adopt enterprisewide architecture, interoperability frameworks, and shared digital platforms and networks, for the whole government. This requires the adoption of common standards for all agencies to integrate their data, business processes, and service delivery applications and channels. One important tool to realize economies of scale and customer-centered government is to organize common business processes across agencies and around user needs. A second practice is to develop a single integrated transactional portal for government services, and to have the portal evolve in response to citizen needs and experiences. A third is to use cloud computing for standard services components to achieve flexibility and fast deployment.

Adopt process transformation practices when putting public services online. Much of the digital dividends of ICT come from business-process-reengineering (BPR) and innovation, not just automation of existing processes and practices. BPR practice has spread widely in the business sector, but not yet in the public service sector—due to the risk-averse culture of public bureaucracies, weak social demand for accountability, and the absence of competition in public service delivery. These challenges to process transformation are particularly strong in developing countries. To counter them, DFGG and for process and service improvements should be strengthened in advance or in conjunction with putting services online.

Mobilize demand and monitor adoption of e-services. Unlocking the potential of e-government depends on high-levels of uptake of e-services. Mobilizing demand and educating users are greater challenges in developing countries where there is little awareness among the masses and low ICT literacy. Marketing of people-friendly websites, development of a single e-government brand, and a consistent navigation with a common look and feel are a best practice. Demand-side metrics should be designed to track the use of, and satisfaction with, e-government. Supply-side metrics can include benchmarks such as availability of portals and applications, sophistication of functionality; and management performance benchmarks such as measurements of government progress toward stated goals. Most indicators can be captured through Internet surveys. Better understanding of how to attract, engage, and incentivize citizens is needed to bridge the gap between putting services online and the service being used. Strengthening DFGG and increasing the "voice of the user" in e-service planning can also help.

Secure complementary reforms when automating public services. Complementary and aligned sectoral policies and incentives are essential to realize a service's digital transformation potential. For public services, the key complementary factors are leadership, accountability, and governance within the sector, and effective citizens' demand and participation. Automation of services must be accompanied by changes as may be needed in laws and management practices, business process simplification, regulatory and administrative reforms, and capacity building for service users and managers. ICT can be used to strengthen these complementary factors, for example by facilitating transparency, citizen feedback, and online monitory of service delivery.

Take account of institutional conditions, and amenability of service to monitoring and citizen participation. The impact of digital technology on citizen empowerment and government capability to improve services depends on the initial strengths of public institutions, and complementary investments in them. For services that are hard to monitor and require more discretion from workers, such as health and educational services, the quality of institutions is more important. Policy makers and administrators need to have the incentives to make the necessary changes. Digital technologies, aligned with incentives of politicians, public administrators, and service providers can be highly effective in improving services. Sustained collective action is often necessary to overcome these institutional constraints. This understanding of institutional conditions and service amenability to monitoring and citizen feedback should guide the selection, phasing and improvement of public services.

5. Deploy Supply and Demand Measures Synergistically

   Act on both supply and demand measures synergistically. Measures to improve public service via e-government have tended to focus on supply-side measures. Only more recently demand-side measures (led by citizens and CSOs) have been considered. Greater emphasis should be placed on joint state–civil society initiatives, and on finding synergistic ways to act on both supply and demand measures. Various social accountability mechanisms have originated from CSOs and some originated from official state bodies, but also, crucially, some have come from governments and CSOs working in tandem, which have tended to be most effective in sustained improvements in service delivery.

   Progress in drawing on open government data and on ICT for demand-driven service improvement rests on supply-strengthening, first-generation e-government strategies, to digitize government processes, populate government databases with timely and reliable data, and develop channels for citizen-centric service delivery. Unfortunately, developing countries still have a long way to go in implementing these first-generation e-government strategies, in parallel with first-generation public-sector reforms. The promise associated with the fast diffusion of mobile and social networks as tools for demand-driven governance may be false or short-lived, if digital transformation of government processes and a culture of openness are not advanced in tandem.

Fortunately, if appropriately designed, ICT applications in government can strengthen both the supply and demand sides of service improvement. For example, government e-procurement can both contribute to timely and accurate information on procurement opportunities, increased competition among potential suppliers, and improved transparency in decisions about final awards—leading to smart procurement decisions, improved procurement policies and practices, and enhanced transparency and oversight.

Use a DFGG lens to prioritize investments in e-services and secure continuous improvement. E-government strategies should aim to improve public sector management and the supply of services, while crafting information and communication systems that deepen transparency and accountability. Improvements in the technological base of service delivery sectors should aim to promote both efficiency (including access, quality, and cost of service) and accountability (by enhancing access to information for policy makers, administrators, and consumers).

Sequence e-government and ICT for DFGG to facilitate openness from the start. Different stages of digitization of services and governance may call for different sequencing strategies. Where both are at evenly advanced stages, both sides should be pursued jointly, as this would broaden ownership by strengthening demand from CSOs for further improvements in ICT-enabled public services and at the same time, by positioning policy makers and service providers to respond to these demands most effectively. Where e-government programs are at early stages and far behind the rising expectations and level of DFGG, it may be prudent to emphasize e-government programs, encourage public–private participation in e-services, and design systems that would phase openness and sharing. Where e-government is at an advanced stage but has been top-down and supply-driven, without adequate DFGG measures, it should become a priority to focus on DFGG and to leverage ICT investments already made in government and service provision so as to improve accountability.

Adopt a phased approach to open government in line with capabilities and level of digitization. The experience of leading adopters of e-government and open government data suggests that open

government builds on already advanced infrastructures for information sharing, data quality, and citizen engagement. Open government thus builds on earlier phases in transforming government
toward a client-centered and service culture—moving to higher
levels of transparency, public participation, and collaboration and
partnerships. This suggests that a phased approach toward open government is a more realistic approach than a complete leapfrogging
or instant paradigm shift.

6. Balance Short- and Long-term Strategies for Scaling Up and
Sustainability

*Lay the ground early on for scaling up and sustainability while sup-
porting small initiatives and quick wins.* Public agencies and service
providers may consider balancing their portfolio of initiatives so as
to create demonstration effects and quick wins on the one hand,
while building the foundations for large-scale transformation and
sustainable impact on services, on the other.

Many ICT-enabled accountability and services improvement
initiatives are developed by communities and local NGOs who get
mobilized in times of crisis but lack the financial strengths needed to
sustain or take initiatives to scale. It will be important to explore how
to scale up successful initiatives at a country level, and how to institutionalize these initiatives in both the government and civil society
for sustainability. This requires balancing the need to demonstrate
quick results in the short term with taking a long-term perspective to
ensure sustainability and appropriate scaling up and impact.

*Governments and aid agencies should aim to amplify and complement
the evolutionary steps of NGOs.* The future of ICT for service improvement and governance will likely consist for the most part not of
"big bang" solutions but rather tens of thousands of more incremen-
tal and tailored efforts in which the locally grounded use of digital
technologies helps to provide information and facilitate communication that civil society groups and governments can use to enhance
their current efforts to make the government more accountable and
responsive. Aid agencies, working closely with governments and
CSOs, should seek to align the socio-technical innovations of ICT
with specific long-term governance improvement objectives. Such

alignment would ensure that socio-technical innovations would have maximum impact, secure complementary investments, lead to cumulative learning, and sustain long-term reforms.

Nurture an enabling environment for long-term strategies. This may include a variety of measures. First, mobilize public opinion (through traditional and new media) for accountability and better public services. Second, develop long-term strategies and institutions to lay the foundation for many ICT-enabled governance initiatives and social innovations at the grassroots level. Third, prioritize and open up government data to external actors, and promote platforms such as crowdsourcing and mobile phones. Fourth, organize service user groups to strengthen demand and contribute to continuous service improvement.

7. Address the Enabling Environment and Ecosystem of the ICT Sector
   Address systemic constraints. As opportunities for micro-interventions to use mobile and other ICT tools multiply, it becomes increasingly important for governments and development partners to identify and analyze barriers to greater adoption, scaling up, and sustainability. Large players should focus on addressing systemic factors: availability and cost of bandwidth, digital divide, interoperability standards, IT and change management skills, legal and regulatory environment, public–private partnership practices, e-leadership institutions, evaluative research and the sharing of best practices, among others.
   Focus on overall functioning of the ICT ecosystem so as to support mobile-phone networks, shared access centers, and local content; and promote partnerships among actors. Governments and their major development partners should be focused on the overall functioning of the ICT ecosystem. For example, such an approach would promote ecosystems that support and take advantage of mobile phones and networks, social media, and digital mapping technologies to improve transparency, participation, and service delivery. It would promote partnerships among NGOs/CSOs, software developers, mobile operators, and government/service providers in search of sustainable business models for mobile apps on DFGG. It would also promote sharing governmentwide digital platforms, e-service delivery channels, open government data, and digital identification.

Develop ICT governance in the public sector to facilitate transparency and service delivery. E-government and ICT governance practices in the public sector exert major influence on the evolution and functioning of the national and local ICT ecosystems. ICT policies and governance should be designed so as to facilitate information sharing, open government, and seamless interactions with citizens across all platforms.

8. Integrate Pro-Poor Policies into ICT for Governance and Service Innovation

Diagnose the sociopolitical context for the pro-poor initiatives. This may involve conducting participatory needs assessments related to empowerment, opportunity, and security of poor people in order to develop ICT applications and tools that would be highly responsive and fit to context. This diagnosis may also assess how the media and other communication channels are representative of the concerns of the poor, so as to provide a basis for targeted interventions to strengthen ICT-enabled services and DFGG for the poor.

Raise awareness and engage pro-poor intermediaries. Awareness raising and capacity building of pro-poor forums and intermediary institutions should be strengthened to secure their effective participation in service improvement and DFGG. It is also important to mobilize and engage poor communities and pro-poor intermediaries in upstream policy dialogue on services and programs of high priority to the poor and for which improved governance and services are critical.

Target key elements of the ICT ecosystem for pro-poor service innovation and governance. Many elements of the ICT ecosystem can bridge the digital divide and participation by the poor and their intermediaries in holding their government accountable to their service priorities and needs. The following are some of the measures to develop the key elements of this ecosystem:

- Adopt a community approach to ICT access, using multistakeholder partnerships to reach the poor. Use community-based ICT centers to organize poor communities, expand their social networks, and raise their digital literacy. Use least-cost subsidy schemes to ensure access costs are affordable.

- Develop local content in local languages.
- Promote the adoption of free/open-source solutions (FOSS) in government and CSOs.
- Liberalize and fast-track licensing of community-based electronic media, particularly community radio.
- Blend "old" ICTs (including radio) with the "latest" (including mobile and Internet) to reach diverse audiences including the poor.
- Embed ICT for service improvement and governance into poverty-reduction programs and strategies.

9. Conduct Research, Learn by Doing, and Capture and Share Best Practices

Emphasize monitoring and evaluation. Rigorous research is needed to assess and improve the potential of e-government and mobile-phone applications. The effects of new technology cannot be fully appreciated by focusing on successful cases alone; successes and failures need to be understood, analyzed, and documented. Policy makers and service providers need to understand the impact of mobile applications, blogs, wikis, and social media, and how they are enabled by national governance and ICT ecosystems. They need to research the enabling policies and institutions to scale, diffuse, and sustain successful ICT uses for service improvement and governance.

Prioritize research on enabling policies and institutions. Giving due attention to scaling up and sustainability raises many critical issues for research: what kinds of enabling policies and institutions are necessary for scaling up and sustaining promising socio-technical innovations for service innovation? How can DFGG remain ahead of the countermoves of repressive governments? What capacity will be needed by CSOs and other politically weak stakeholders to sustain ICT-enabled service improvement, at appropriate scale? What kind of brokering role can governments and aid agencies play to connect the dynamic demand side of civil society and the for-profit ICT sector? Such learning should be jointly pursued by practitioners in the governance, ICT, e-government, and various service sectors.

Capture tacit knowledge from experimenting in different contexts. Although successful examples exist, the "how" of the use of ICT for public service improvement and governance is still not widely practiced in developing countries. There is a lot of excitement about the possibilities opened by mobile phones and crowdsourcing, among other advances. But much of the global stock of knowledge has been developed from engagements in strengthening the supply side of e-government in developed countries. Learning from grassroots practitioners and communities requires aid agencies and central governments to engage with implementing partners and communities involved in the feedback loop. They would also benefit from global and South–South exchanges and partnerships. All partners need to learn systematically and quickly to leverage the fast-moving technologies for the public good.

Bibliography

Acemoglu, D., and Robinson, J. 2012. *Why Nations Fail*. New York: Crown Publishers.

Agarwal, S., and Labrique, A. 2014. "Newborn Health on the Line: The Potential of mHealth Applications." *JAMA* 322, no. 3, p. 2.

Aker, J. 2010. "Dial 'A' for Agriculture: A Review of Information and Communication Technologies for Agricultural Extension in Developing Countries." www.e-agriculture.org/content/dial-agriculture.

Aker, J., and Ksoll, C. 2015. "Call Me Educated: Evidence from a Mobile Monitoring Experiment in Niger" *Working paper no 406*. Center for Global Development, Washington, DC.

Arnold, A. 2011. "Communication Technologies for Accountability." In *Accountability through Public Opinion*, eds. Odugbemi, S., and Lee, T. pp. 1–7. Washington, DC: World Bank.

A T Kearney. 2013. *The Mobile Economy, 2013*. London, UK: A T Kearney.

Ayer, V., Claasen, M., and Alpín-Lardíes, C. 2010. *Social Accountability in Africa: Practitioners' Experiences and Lessons. Idasa & ANSA-Africa*. Cape Town, South Africa: Lobby Books.

Bhatti, Z., Kusek, J., and Verheijen, T. 2015. *Logged on: Smart Government Solutions from South Asia*. Washington, DC: World Bank.

Blair, H. 2011. "Gaining State Support for Social Accountability." In *Accountability through Public Opinion*, eds. Odugbemi, S., and Lee, T. 37–51. Washington, DC: World Bank.

Brin, D. 2011. "The Transparent Society, and Other Articles about Transparency and Privacy." www.davidbrin.com/transparent.htm.

Cantens, T., Raballand, G., Strychacz, N., and Tchouawou, T. 2011. *Reforming African Customs: The Results of the Cameroonian Performance Contract Pilot. Africa Trade Policy Notes No.13*. Washington, DC: World Bank.

Castro, D. 2010. "What's Next for Open Government." *Web Memo*. Washington, DC: The Information Technology and Innovation Foundation.

Chuhan-Pole, P., and Angwafo, M. 2011. *Yes, Africa Can: Success Stories from a Dynamic Continent*. Washington, DC: World Bank.

Claasen, M., Alpín-Lardíes, C., and Ayer, V., eds. 2010. *Social Accountability in Africa: Practitioner's Experiences and Lessons*. Cape Town, South Africa: Affiliated Network for Social Accountability (ANSA-Africa), ABC Press.

CTA (Technical Centre for Agricultural and Rural Cooperation). 2009. "Access and Channels." http://observatory2009.cta.int/wiki/bin/view/Main /AccessAndChannels.

de Lange, J. "TRAC.fm—Public Monitoring of Service Delivery." TRAC Development Consultants.

Demombynes, G., and Romeo, A. *Results from the Southern Sudan Experimental Phone Survey December 2010 Round.* Washington, DC: World Bank.

Dhaliwall, I., and Hanna, R. 2014. "Deal with the Devil: The Success and Limitations of Bureaucratic Reform in India" *National Bureau of Economic Research Working Paper no 20482.*

Eggers, W. 2005. *Government 2.0.* Maryland, MD: Rowman &Littlefield Publishers.

Ekine, S. 2009. *SMS Uprising—Mobile Activism in Africa.* Nairobi, Kenya: Pambazuka Press.

Freeland, N., and Vincent K. 2009. "Upwardly Mobile: The potential to Deliver Social Protection by Cell Phone in Lesotho" in Perspective Proceedings of 1st International Conference on M4D 2008.

FinAccess 2009. "FinAccess National Survey 2009—Dynamics of Kenya's changing financial land scape". www2.Centralbank.go.ke/downloads/publications /general/finaccess.pdf

Fung, R., Gilman, H., and Shkabatur, J. 2010. "Technology for Transparency: The Role of Technology and Citizen Media in Promoting Transparency, Accountability, and Civic Participation." http://globalvoicesonline.org /wpcontent/uploads/2010/05/Technology_for_Transparency.pdf.

Gerster, R., and Zimmerman, S. 2005. *Upscaling Pro-poor ICT-Policies and Practices.* Berne, Switzerland: Swiss Agency for International Development and Cooperation, and M.S. Swaminathan Research Foundation.

Gotez, A., and Jenkins, R. 2005. *Reinventing Accountability: Making Democracy Work for Human Development.* London, UK: Palgrave Macmillan.

Goetz, A., and Jenkins, R. 2011. "Hybrid forms of accountability: citizen engagement in institutions of public Sector oversight in India." *Public Management Review,* no. 3, pp. 363–383.

Ghannam, J. 2011. *Social Media in the Arab World: Leading Up to the Uprising of 2011.* A Report to the Center for International Media Assistance. Washington, DC.

Goldsmith, S. 2010. *The Power of Social Innovation.* San Francisco, CA: Jossey-Bass: Wily Imprint.

Gunaratne, S. 2011. "New Partners in Africa's Development: The Role of India." Paper prepared for Africa Regional Management, World Bank, Washington, DC.

Hanna, N.K. 1991. "The Information Technology Revolution and Economic Development." World Bank Discussion Paper 120, Washington, DC.

Hanna, N.K. 2009. *e-Transformation: Enabling New Development Strategies*. New York: Springer.

Hanna, N.K. 2010. *Transforming Government and Building the Information Society: Challenges and Opportunities for the Developing World*. New York: Springer.

Hanna, N.K. 2011a. *Seeking Transformation through Information Technology: Strategies for Brazil, China, Canada and Sri Lanka*. New York: Springer.

Hanna, N.K. 2011b. *National Strategies to Harness Information Technology: Seeking Transformation in Singapore, Finland, the Philippines, and South Africa*. New York: Springer.

Hanna, N.K. 2012. *Open, Smart, and Inclusive Development: ICT for Transforming North Africa*. Abidjan: African Development Fund. http://zunia.org/fr/post/open-smart-and-inclusive-development-ict-for-transforming-north-africa

Hanna, N.K. 2015. *Transforming to a Networked Society: Guide for Policy Makers*. Gaithersburg, MD: Sriban.

Hanna, N.K. 2016. *Mastering Digital Transformation*. Bingley, UK: Emerald

Hanna, N.K., Guy, K., and Arnold, E. 1995. *Information Technology Diffusion: Experience of IndustriCountries and Lessons for Developing Countries*. World Bank Staff Working Paper. The World Bank, Washington D.C.

Hanna, N.K., Boyson, S., and Gunaratne, S. 1996. *The East Asia Miracle and Information Technology*. Washington, D.C.: World Bank.

Hanna, N.K., and Picciotto, R. 2002. *Making Development Work: Development Learning in a World of Wealth and Poverty*. New Jersey: Transactions Publications.

Hanna, N.K., and Rubino-Hallman, S. 2006. "New Technologies for Public Sector Transformation: A Critical Analysis of e-Government Initiatives in Latin America and the Caribbean." *Journal e Govern* 3, no. 3, pp. 3–39.

Hanna, N.K., and Qiang, C. 2009. "Trends in National E-Government Institutions." In *Information and Communications for Development 2009: Extending Reach and Increasing Impact*. Washington, DC: World Bank.

Hellström, J. 2009. "Mobile Democracy—Challenges and Way Forward." In *Big Brother and Empowered Sisters—The Role of New Communication Technologies in Democratic Processes*, eds. Rudebeck, L., Hellström, J., and Melin, M. Uppsala, Sweden: Uppsala University. http://upgraid.files.wordpress.com/2009/11/kus_bok31.pdf.

Hellström, J. 2010. "The Innovative Use of Mobile Applications in East Africa." *Sida Review 2010*, p. 12. http://upgraid.files.wordpress.com/2010/06/sr2010-12_sida_hellstrom.pdf.

IEA (International Energy Agency). 2008. "The Electricity Access Database." www.iea.org/weo/database_electricity/electricity_access_database.htm.

Intelecon. 2011. "Mobile Applications for Rural Development." Presentation by Intelecon to the World Bank, Washington, DC, January 20.

Jenkins, R. 2011. "Embedding the Right to Information: The Uses of Sector-Specific Transparency Regimes." In *Accountability through Public Opinion*, eds. Odugbemi, S., and Lee, T. pp. 403–412. Washington, DC: World Bank.

Joyce, M.C. 2010. "Reflecting on Tech for Transparency." Blogpost. www.meta-activism.org/2010/09/reflecting-on-tech-for-transparency/. (date accessed September 15, 2010).

Kasozi, R. 2010. "Ministry of ICT: Do They Have a Budget for Website Maintenance?" Mail posted September 11, 2010, to i-network@dgroups.org.

Kpundeh, S., Khadiagala, G., and Chowdhury, S., eds. 2008. *Information and Service Delivery: Case Studies from Kenya and Ethiopia.* Washington, DC: Africa Region, World Bank.

Kreutz, C. 2011. "Mobile Activism in Africa: Future Trends and Software Developments." In *SMS Uprising—Mobile Activism in Africa*, ed. Ekine, S. Oxford,UK: Fahamu Books & Pambazuka Press.

Lampathaki, F., Charalabidis, Y., Passas, S., et al. 2014. "Defining a Taxonomy for Research Areas on ICT for Governance and Policy Modelling." https://hal.inria.fr/hal-01059163.

Lee, T. 2011. "The (Im)Possibility of Mobilizing Public Opinion?" In *Accountability through Public Opinion*, eds. Odugbemi, S., and Lee, T. pp. 11–23. Washington, DC: World Bank.

Lee, G., and Kwak, Y.H. 2011. *An Open Government Implementation Model: Moving to Increased Public Engagement.* Washington, DC: IBM Center for the Business of Government.

Mahoney, M.S., and Webley, P. 2004. *The Impact of Transparency: A Cross-National Study.* Exeter, UK: School of Psychology, University of Exeter. www.fig.net/news/archive/news_2004/mahoney_webley.pdf.

Mail and Guardian Online. 2010. "Mozambique Govt Suspends SMSes." www.mg.co.za/article/2010-09-11-mozambique-govt-suspends-smses. (date accessed September 11, 2010.)

McNeil, M., and Malena, C. 2010. *Demanding Good Governance—Lessons from Social Accountability Initiatives in Africa.* Washington, DC: World Bank. https://openknowledge.worldbank.org/bitstream/handle/10986/2478/5554 60PUB0Dema1EPI1978968101PUBLIC1.pdf;sequence=1

Minister of Government Policy. 2011. *Open Public Service White Paper.* United Kingdom: Minister of Government Policy.

Odugbemi, S. 2011. "The Public and Its (Alleged) Handiwork." In *Accountability through Public Opinion*, eds. Odugbemi, S., and Lee, T. pp. 25–34. Washington, DC: World Bank.

Odugbemi, S., and T. Lee. 2011. "Taking Direct Accountability Seriously." In *Accountability through Public Opinion*, eds. Odugbemi, S., and Lee, T. pp. 1–7. Washington, DC: World Bank.

Odugbemi, S., and Lee, T. 2011. *Accountability Through Public Opinion.* Washington, DC: World Bank.

Odugbemi, S., and Jacobson, T. 2008. *Governance Reform under Real-World Conditions.* Washington, DC: World Bank.

OpenNet Initiative. 2009. "Internet Filtering in Sub-Saharan Africa." http://opennet.net/sites/opennet.net/files/ONI_SSAfrica_2009.pdf.

Open Society Foundation, Transparency and Accountability Initiative. 2011. *Opening Government.* London, UK: Open Society Foundation.

Poverty Reduction and Economic Management (PREM). 2011. "Strengthening Public Financial Management in Post Conflict Countries." In *Economic Premise,* eds. Fritz, V., Hedger, E., and Lopes, A.P. p. 54, Washington, DC: World Bank.

Roberts, A. 2010. *The Logic of the Discipline: Global Capitalism and the Architecture of Government.* New York: Oxford University Press.

Safaricom. 2009. *Press Release—M-PESA in Partnership with Grundfos for Rural Water Provision.* September 4, 2009. www.safaricom.co.ke/fileadmin/template/main/downloads/m-pesa_resource_centre/M-PESA_Press%20Briefs/09.09.06%20-%20Grundfos%20Launch.pdf.

Sasaki, D., ed. 2010. *Technology for Transparency—The Role of Technology and Citizen Media in Promoting Transparency, Accountability and Civic Participation.* Technology for Transparency Network. http://globalvoicesonline.org/wp-content/uploads/2010/05/Technology_for_Transparency.pdf.

Schuster, C., and Brito, C. 2011. "Cutting costs, boosting quality and collecting data real-time –Lessons from a Cell Phone-Based Beneficiary Survey to Strengthen Guatemala's Conditional Cash Transfer Program. *en breve* Latin America Region." World Bank. www.worldbank.org/enbreve.

Shirky, C. 2011. "The Political Power of Social Media." *Foreign Affairs,* February 2011.

Srivastava, V., and Marco, L. 2011. "Decentralization in Post-Conflict Sierra Leone: The Genie is out of the Bottle." World Bank, Washington, DC.

Stanford Social Innovation Review. 2011. "Crowdsourcing Microfinance." *Stanford Soc Innov Rev* 9, no. 3, pp. 70–72.

Tactical Technology Collective. 2008. "Mobiles in-a-Box." https://mobiles.tacticaltech.org/.

Tapscott, D., and Williams, A. 2010. *MacroWikinomics: Rebooting Business and the World.* New York: Penguin Group.

The Economist. 2009. "Mobile Marvels: A Special Report on Telecoms in Emerging Markets." www.economist.com/specialreports/displayStory.cfm?story_id=14483896.

Yonazi, E., Kelly, T., Halewood N., and Blackman, C (Eds). 2012. *The Transformational Use of Information and Communication Technologies in Africa.* World Bank, African Development Bank, and African Union.

UN (United Nations) 2008. *World e-Parliament Report.* New York: United Nations.

West, D. 2005. *Digital Government.* New Jersey: Princeton University Press.

World Bank. 2001. *World Development Report 2001: Attacking Poverty.* Washington, DC: World Bank

World Bank. 2003. *World Development Report 2004—Making Services Work for Poor People.*https://openknowledge.worldbank.org/handle/10986/5986

World Bank. 2005. *Building Effective States, Forging Engaged Societies.* Report of the World Bank Task Force on Capacity Development in Africa. http://siteresources.worldbank.org/EXTAFRDEVOPRTSK/Resources/acdtf_report.pdf.

World Bank. 2007a. *Strengthening World Bank Group Engagement on Governance and Anti-Corruption.* http://siteresources.worldbank.org/EXTPUBLICSEC TORANDGOVERNANCE/Resources/GACStrategyPaper.pdf.

World Bank. 2007b. *Social Accountability—Enhancing Citizen Voice and Client Focus in Governance and Service Delivery.* www.worldbank.org.kh/pecsa /resources/sa_enhancing_citizen_voice.pdf.

World Bank. 2008. "Strengthening WBG Engagement on Governance and Anti-Corruption: Year One Implementation." A presentation delivered during the 2008 annual meetings, Washington, DC. http://siteresources.worldbank.org/ PUBLICSECTORANDGOVERNANCE/Resources/GACProgress.ppt.

World Bank. 2011a. *Shifting the Balance: Rethinking the World Bank's Engagement on Demand for Good Governance (DFGG).* Draft dated February 2011. Washington, DC: World Bank.

World Bank. 2011b. *Empowering Africans to Hold Their Governments Accountable: An AFR Strategy to Support Demand for Good Governance.* Washington, DC: World Bank.

World Bank. 2012. *eTransform Africa: The Transformational use of Information and Communications Technologies in Africa.* Washington, DC: World Bank.

World Bank. 2015. *MajiVoice: A New Accountability Tool to Improve Public Services.* Washington, DC: World Bank.

World Bank. 2016. *Digital Dividends. World Development Report 2016.* Washington, DC: World Bank

World Bank. 2017. *Governance and the Law. World Development Report 2017.* Washington, DC: World Bank

World Bank Institute. 2005. *Social Accountability in the Public Sector. A Conceptual Discussion and Learning Module.* Washington, DC: World Bank.

World Bank Institute. 2010. *Cell Phones and Radio Counter Corruption in Burundi.* Washington, DC: World Bank. http://wbi.worldbank.org/wbi /stories/cell-phones-and-radio-counter-corruption-burundi.

Yilmaz, F., and Coolidge, J. 2013. "Can E-Filing Reduce Tax Compliance Costs in Developing Countries?" *World Bank Policy Research Paper no. 6647.*

Index

OTHER TITLES IN OUR SERVICE SYSTEMS AND INNOVATIONS IN BUSINESS AND SOCIETY COLLECTION

Jim Spohrer, IBM and Haluk Demirkan, Arizona State University, *Editors*

- *Collaborative Innovation: How Clients and Service Providers Can Work By Design to Achieve It by* Tony Morgan
- *Sustainable Service* by Adi Wolfson
- *Fair Pay: Adaptively Win-Win Customer Relationships* by Richard Reisman
- *Business Engineering and Service Design, Second Edition* by Oscar Barros
- *Service Design with Applications to Health Care Institutions* by Oscar Barros
- *Obtaining Value from Big Data for Service Delivery* by Stephen H. Kaisler, Frank Armour, and William Money
- *Service Innovation* by Anders Gustafsson, Per Kristensson, Gary R. Schirr, and Lars Witell
- *Matching Services to Markets: The Role of the Human Sensorium in Shaping Service-Intensive Markets* by H.B. Casanova
- *Achieving Success through Innovation: Cases and Insights from the Hospitality, Travel, and Tourism Industry* by Glenn Withiam
- *Designing Service Processes to Unlock Value, Second Edition* by Joy M. Field
- *Citizen-Centered Cities, Volume I: Case Studies of Public Involvement* by Paul R. Messinger
- *Citizen-Centered Cities, Volume II: City Studies of Public Involvement* by Paul R. Messinger

Announcing the Business Expert Press Digital Library

Concise e-books business students need for classroom and research

This book can also be purchased in an e-book collection by your library as

- a one-time purchase,
- that is owned forever,
- allows for simultaneous readers,
- has no restrictions on printing, and
- can be downloaded as PDFs from within the library community.

Our digital library collections are a great solution to beat the rising cost of textbooks. E-books can be loaded into their course management systems or onto students' e-book readers.
The **Business Expert Press** digital libraries are very affordable, with no obligation to buy in future years. For more information, please visit **www.businessexpertpress.com/librarians**. To set up a trial in the United States, please email **sales@businessexpertpress.com**.

CPSIA information can be obtained
at www.ICGtesting.com
Printed in the USA
BVOW11s2110230417
481971BV00005B/38/P